'26/14
UBT
4,95

D0226236

The Complete Guide to
Professional
Networking

The Complete Guide to
Professional
Networking

The secrets of online and offline success

Simon Phillips
with cartoons and caricatures by
Simon Ellinas

KoganPage

LONDON PHILADELPHIA NEW DELHI

MASTICS-MORICHES-SHIRLEY
COMMUNITY LIBRARY

Publisher's note

Every possible effort has been made to ensure that the information contained in this book is accurate at the time of going to press, and the publishers and authors cannot accept responsibility for any errors or omissions, however caused. No responsibility for loss or damage occasioned to any person acting, or refraining from action, as a result of the material in this publication can be accepted by the editor, the publisher or any of the authors.

First published in Great Britain and the United States in 2014 by Kogan Page Limited

Apart from any fair dealing for the purposes of research or private study, or criticism or review, as permitted under the Copyright, Designs and Patents Act 1988, this publication may only be reproduced, stored or transmitted, in any form or by any means, with the prior permission in writing of the publishers, or in the case of reprographic reproduction in accordance with the terms and licences issued by the CLA. Enquiries concerning reproduction outside these terms should be sent to the publishers at the undermentioned addresses:

2nd Floor, 45 Gee Street	1518 Walnut Street, Suite 1100	4737/23 Ansari Road
London EC1V 3RS	Philadelphia PA 19102	Daryaganj
United Kingdom	USA	New Delhi 110002
		India

www.koganpage.com

© Simon Phillips (writer) and Simon Ellinas (cartoonist), 2014

The right of Simon Phillips and Simon Ellinas to be identified as the authors of this work has been asserted by them in accordance with the Copyright, Designs and Patents Act 1988.

ISBN 978 0 7494 6891 0
E-ISBN 978 0 7494 6892 7

British Library Cataloguing-in-Publication Data

A CIP record for this book is available from the British Library.

Library of Congress Cataloging-in-Publication Data

Phillips, Simon (Business networking consultant)
    The complete guide to professional networking : the secrets of online and offline success / Simon Phillips and Simon Ellinas.
        pages cm
        ISBN 978-0-7494-6891-0 (paperback) — ISBN 978-0-7494-6892-7 (ebook)
    1. Business networks. 2. Businesspeople. 3. Online social networks. 4. Interpersonal relations.
    I. Ellinas, Simon. II. Title.
        HD69.S8.P5135 2014
        650.1′3—dc23
                                                                                2014014072

Typeset by Amnet
Printed and bound in India by Replika Press, Pvt Ltd

We would like to dedicate this book to the networks of people in the charitable and social enterprise sectors who work tirelessly every day to make a difference to the lives of their fellow human beings.

Contents

NIGEL RISNER!

I ♥ NETWORKING

Simon Ollinas
caricatures.org.uk
07790 393239

Foreword

You have to do it by yourself and you cannot do it alone
This book is written with one goal in mind
To help you increase your net worth by increasing your
network

There are many how to books, but very few with practical tips
and secrets that give you the competitive edge
What Simon has done is take all his knowledge and spoken to
the best networkers around the world to give you the definitive
guide to making you as connected as you can be

You need to read the book once
Go and do the stuff he shares
Re-read the book and then do it properly
If you want to support your friends to give them the chance to
succeed, don't lend them yours – go and buy them a copy

This book shouldn't be placed on the bookshelf; it needs to be
carried with you as a reminder that you and you alone have to
go and get connected. But you will need a network to realize
your dreams if you want to fast track in this highly competitive
world

Have fun networking and remember every one you ever
wanted to meet is in your or your friends' network

Nigel Risner
www.nigelrisner.com

Acknowledgements: Behind the scenes of a networked book

> *None of us got to where we are alone. Whether the assistance we received was obvious or subtle, acknowledging someone's help is a big part of understanding the importance of saying thank you.*
>
> Harvey Mackay, author of Swimming with Sharks

I decided to write a book on networking because I see it as one of three essential skills to help you survive and thrive in today's society. The other two skills are using your time effectively and dealing with change. All three come together in a development programme called JoinTheGreats. Although I've been networking for most of my adult life (and unknowingly since I was about 4), I knew that I was not an expert in any of the key aspects that I wanted to discuss in this book. I had experience in all of the areas, but as a result of the networks I have built, I knew that there were real experts out there that, if I could persuade them to become involved, would be able to provide you with a wealth of great advice, ideas and successful strategies to help you move on quicker. With this approach in mind, I drew up a dream list of who I would like to interview for the book and quickly landed on about two dozen names of globally recognized experts in my network that I would love to involve. However, as I started to make the phone calls, the list of potential interviewees grew and grew as my contacts began to identify people in their networks that I should talk to. I wasn't surprised; after all, these are people with massive networks, but I was overwhelmed by their generosity and enthusiasm to get involved. Many of them were thrilled that someone was going to attempt to make the world of networking more accessible and less intimidating for everyone.

Although many of them are quoted in the book and I have shared their contact details with you, not one of them asked me to do this. Many of them, at their own expense of time and money, met with me for a live, filmed interview and still no demands, or even subtle hints, of expected reward. From my perspective though, referring them to you, through this book, is the least I could do for them and the best thing I can do for you, to help you in your further research. I can recommend every single person involved in the book and have done so many times already outside of this piece of work.

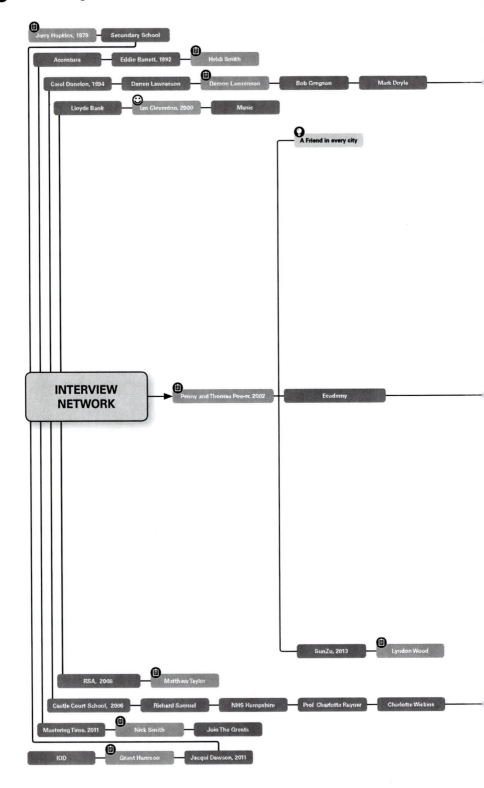

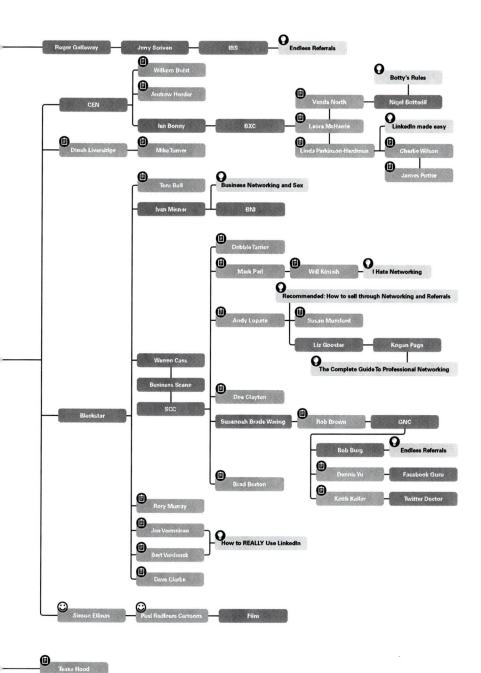

As the diagram on the preceding two pages shows, my interviewees included someone I met on my first day of secondary school in 1979. I did not know then that my friend Jerry Hopkins would be a valuable piece of the jigsaw in creating this book. However, Jerry's experience of building effective networks within organizations was pivotal to the thinking for Chapter 7 – a great example of digging your well before you need it. Only in a professional sense of course, Jerry's friendship over the years has been just as valuable.

Moving forward in time, I met a whole bunch of wonderful people in 1996–2000 through a direct marketing business that I was building. The team of people I worked with were second to none in their commitment to develop themselves so that they could help the team around them and I learned a lot just through my association with them. I am fortunate enough to count many of them as close friends today and their success in a variety of fields, aided by effective networking, gave me a fortunate opportunity to catch up with them for this book.

In 2000, I started Simesco and met my business bank manager for the first time, Ian Cleverdon. Clev is one of those super talented individuals you come across every now and again in life, who seems to be able to turn his hand to most things. As well as being a great sounding board to me in my early days in business, Ian has scored many pieces of music for big corporates, performs as part of folk duo The Huers and has even found time to record some work for me. Cheers Ian.

In 2002, as part of the research for my first book, *Time Management 24/7*, I became aware of a relatively small group of individuals that were forging ahead with the idea of networking online. In particular, I bought a book called *A Friend in Every City* by someone called Thomas Power who was working with his wife Penny Power to bring to life her vision of a support network for people who were not working within the traditional confines of an office. Their social business network, Ecademy, was a forerunner to many of the online platforms that we all know and use today and introduced me to a network of innovative, supportive and relationship-focused individuals that, as you can see from the diagram, are still pioneering in their fields today. We all learned a lot from Penny and Thomas and continue to do so today.

Ecademy was the home of my first personal professional network, the CEN. This group of consultants, trainers and coaches grew to well over 700 members from across the globe which, before the advent of the Group functionality on LinkedIn, was the largest network of its kind in the world. The relationships I formed at this time, through the CEN and BlackStar (which was a life membership group on Ecademy), have sustained me through some of the toughest times in my life and it is so great to see so many of them building networked businesses and reputations that match their incomparable character. Thanks in particular to William Buist, Andrew Horder, Bev Hamilton, Derek and Jo Bishop, Tom Ball, Ivan Misner, Judith Germain, Jan Vermeiren, Dave Clarke, Michael Don Smith, Rob Hook, Daniel Priestley, Mike Turner, Dinah Liversidge, Griselda Mussett, Christine Miller, Stephen Harvard Davies, Fraser Hay, Mindy Gibbins-Klein, Donnie McNicol, Rory Murray, Stella Hollman, Anne Andrews, Mark Lee, Tom Evans, Andrew Widgery, Andrew Wilcox, Malcolm Tullett, Andrew Preston, Andy Lopata, Nick Heap and last but not least Victoria Bullis.

The second network I created was called South Coast Connections which I imagined while working with the inimitable Warren Cass, as one of the regional directors of Business Scene. I wanted to find a way of bringing together all of the different networking groups that were sprouting up all around us in Dorset and Hampshire and, with the help of some fantastic people, we managed to create some great events that continue to this day, thanks to the effervescent Debbie Tarrier and now Warren himself. Genuine heartfelt thanks to Laura McHarrie, Steve Graham, Emma James, Helen Jeffery, Alan Adair, Andy Clarke, Christopher Jones and James Lattimer.

Over the past eight years, as a privileged countryman of Aneurin Bevan, it has been an honour to work alongside the many wonderful people in the UK's National Health Service. I have also ventured into the pioneering sphere of social enterprise. These two aspects of my life have brought me into contact with some amazing people, as you would imagine. There are far too many to list them all, but most will understand if I highlight James Rose, Kathy Toop, Gabriele Prestidge, Christina Bush, Kevin Garrett, Caroline Des Rivieres, Charlotte Rayner, Cliff Ferguson, Sue Dovey, Martin Edwards, Cliff Finlay, Lucie Lleshi, Ruth Horton, Richard Clark, Mary Deeks and everyone at NHS Central Southern CSU.

To come right up to date, the following friends deserve a special thank you for supporting me through some pretty tough times in recent years: Vanda North, Susannah Brade Waring, the Mooseketeers, Carol, Tereasa, Lynn and Vicky, Ian and Fran Bonny, Nick Smith, Sue Wellman, Sam Johnson, Jenny Tunley Price, Alison Rogers, Nicky Carew and Jacqui Couzens – I am blessed to have you in my life.

This project has been brought to you thanks to the super drawing talents of Simon Ellinas, the generous contribution of our experts and finally Liz Gooster and Philippa Fiszzon, our gifted, patient and perceptive publishing team.

Networking experts

Name	Description
Andrew Horder	Life coach and author of *The Busy Fool*
Andy Lopata	Best-selling author of *Recommended: How to sell through networking and referrals* and leading business networking strategist
Bert Verdonck	Co-author of *How to Really Use LinkedIn*
Brad Burton	Founder of 4Networking
Charlie Lawson	National Director of Business Networks International in the UK and Ireland
Damon Lawrenson	Award-winning interim Financial Director
Dave Clarke	Founder and CEO of NRG Business Networks
Debbie Tarrier	Former host of South Coast Connections and voice-over artist and presenter
Dennis Yu	Facebook expert and CEO of Blitz Local
Dinah Liversidge	Co-founder of #thebreakfastclub, motivational executive business mentor and author of *The Credibility Curve*
Grant Harrison	Former Chair of the Institute of Directors for Hampshire and the Isle of Wight, and also Board Director of Solent India Business Network
Heidi Smith	Founder and Director of www.russianparalegals.com
James Potter	"The LinkedIn Man" – strategic business advisor
Jan Vermeiren	Co-author of *How to Really Use LinkedIn*
Jeremy Hopkins	Operations Director for Williams Medical Supplies
Keith Keller	Global Twitter Marketing Specialist
Laura McHarrie	Founder of The Entrepreneur Hub and local networking specialist
Linda Parkinson-Hardman	Author of *LinkedIn Made Easy* and founder and CEO of The Hysterectomy Association
Lyndon Wood	Founder of SunZu (formerly Ecademy)
Mark Perl	Trainer in business networking skills, author of *How to Host and Plan Events* and UK LinkedIn trainer
Matthew Taylor	Chief Executive of the RSA
Mike Turner	Managing Director of Music Bus
Rob Brown	Best-selling author of *How to Build Your Reputation* and Head of the Global Networking Council
Susan Mumford	Founder of Be Smart About Art and the Association of Women Art Dealers
Tessa Hood	Personal Brand and Reputation Developer and author of *The Personal Brandwagon (... and how to jump on it)*
Thomas Power	Former Chairman of Ecademy, no. 1 most connected person on LinkedIn and co-founder of Scredible Leaders
Tom Ball	Founder and CEO of NearDesk
Vanda North	Author, speaker, global trainer and mind chi inventor
William Buist	Collaboration specialist, director at Abelard Management Services Limited
Will Kintish	Author of *I Hate Networking*

01

What is networking?

> *Networking is rubbish; have friends instead.*
>
> *Steve Winwood*

Since the first groups came together to interact, share and form social connections, we have been networking. Networking is nothing more than the development of relationships and your personal network can be measured by the number and quality of relationships you have. The effectiveness of your network is further determined by the strength of those same relationships. In fact, everything to do with networking can be viewed through the prism of relationships:

- Effective network = strong relationships.
- Support network = close relationships.
- Collaborative network = mutually beneficial relationships.
- Social network = informal relationships.
- Business network = formal relationships.
- Social business network = balanced relationships.
- Trusted network = reliable and dependable relationships.
- Referral network = informed and motivated relationships.

We're going to talk a lot about the word relationships as we proceed through both this chapter and the book but, for now, have a quick think about who might be in your various networks, as defined above. These groups are not necessarily mutually exclusive, so don't worry if some individuals make more than one appearance.

Definitions

To save you searching online, here are the formal definitions of networking, starting with my favourite:

Creating a group of acquaintances and associates and keeping it active through regular communication for mutual benefit. Networking is based on the question, 'How can I help?' and not with, 'What can I get?'
BusinessDictionary.com

A group or system of interconnected things or people.
The Oxford English Dictionary definition of a (business) network

The informal sharing of information and services among individuals or groups linked by a common interest.
TheFreeDictionary.com

What the experts say

Every single person that we spoke to when researching this book, identified the word 'relationships' as the most critical component of networking. Regardless of the type of networks they were talking about or the activities they were describing, it all came down to 'relationships' as far as they were concerned. Now, that's great news for you because you already have a whole load of relationships in your life, so no-one is starting from scratch; especially in this world of instant and global connectivity; even if you move away from your family and friends, you can remain connected.

There are some differences, but it is usually one of emphasis rather than substance. So, for example, Tom Ball, who we shall meet up with again later in the book, describes networking as:

 Bringing together all of the resources that you need to go to business. So you have some of the skills, some of the money yourself, the rest you have to find through other people.

Tom Ball, founder and CEO of NearDesk

Relationships are still key, but the emphasis has become more specifically focused on solving a business problem and, having known Tom for a number of years, I know that he doesn't look for shortcuts when it comes to helping others.

This focus on creating a personal market for exchanging your talent, connections and opportunities, within the context of strong relationship building, underpins the language of many experts. For example, according to Dr Ivan Misner, networking is:

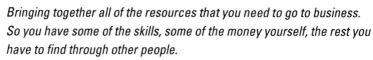 *The process of developing and activating your relationships to increase your business, enhance your knowledge, expand your sphere of influence or serve the community.*

Ivan Misner, Founder of BNI® (Business Network International)

While Donna Fisher captures perfectly the core truth of networking in this description:

 Networking is choosing interdependence over isolation and realizing the power of cooperation over competition – it links people and information to one another for the mutual benefit of everyone involved.

Donna Fisher, speaker and author

The 10 keys to building your network

 It occurs to me that our survival may depend upon our talking to one another.

Dan Simmons, Hyperion

It would appear to be universally agreed that networking is all about building relationships, but what exactly does that mean? After all, we have a relationship of sorts with everyone that we encounter on a day-to-day basis, are they all in our network? The simple answer is 'Yes'. Everyone that you have ever known, know today or will get to know tomorrow is potentially a member of your network, or more accurately networks. The advantage of thinking of everyone in this way is that you will stop trying to 'network' when you meet someone who you think might be a valuable connection and instead you will just focus on making a new friend. If you like to break things down into their constituent parts, our aim when we meet someone new is to interact with them, share some information to get to know them better and forge a real connection. From there, we can choose which network we want to add them to; although, in reality, we don't really get to choose in a clinical way. Relationships develop over time and it is not always clear from our first meeting with someone that they will, for example, become a member of our trusted network. So, the secret is to stop focusing on yourself and your needs and ask yourself, as the BusinessDictionary.com suggested, 'How can I help them?'

With this overall approach in mind, here are 10 steps to building great relationships or networking as some people call it. They are not in a strict order, but it is possible that one of your relationships might follow this sequence.

1 Identifying

Never under-estimate anyone, never over-estimate anyone, treat everyone the same, with respect.

Brad Burton, founder of 4Networking,
author and speaker

Have you ever been in such a hurry to get somewhere that your memory of the journey is a blur? The same can be true if you are searching for that specific someone to move your career forward or provide that perfect connection – you will miss some people that could have been very influential in your life. By all means set yourself a goal of contacting a whole group of people that fall into a specific category or job title if that is what you have decided will further your ambitions, but make sure you enjoy the journey too. You just don't know how some people will influence your life over time. You may determine that the shop owner will be of no benefit to your aspirations of being a DJ on the radio, only to find that their sister is the star presenter on the local station. You can count the number of seeds in the apple, but not the number of apples in the seed.

Assuming you can get over the very human trait of making assumptions and decide to just talk to anyone, there is a benefit in developing a clear picture in your mind of your perfect connection. Who is it that you would most like to meet to take your career to the next level or even help you get started? What is their job title? What sort of organizations do they work in? What jobs did they have prior to getting where they are now? Who do you know that may know them? These days, tools like LinkedIn make this sort of identification process very simple, but it makes sense to ask the people in your offline network too. It gives you something to talk about and provides them with some information on how they may be able to help you.

Armed with this knowledge, you can also start to think through where you are going to spend your time. Are there specific events that these people attend or venues at which they are likely to gather? Do they have an industry body or network you could join? Is there some way you can volunteer to work alongside these individuals and learn how they operate? To turn to the most accessible, is there a specific event that they are attending in your area? These days, as we will see later, there are plenty of events listed online and you can see the profile of attendees before you even set off. Do a bit more research; see if there are any points of obvious connection that you could mention should you meet them.

2 *Connecting*

 Networking is about connecting with people, pure and simple. We start networking as soon as we step foot in school.
Laura McHarrie, founder of The Entrepreneur
Hub and local networking specialist

You can connect with people in many ways. You can follow them on Twitter, add them on Google+, send them a friend request on Facebook or a connect request on LinkedIn. You could say 'Hi' to them while out shopping or bump into them at an industry or family event. Wherever you find people, you will find opportunities to connect. There are individual strategies for connecting with people, online or offline, and we will come to those later. For now, the only thing you need to remember is you will never make a connection unless you attempt to communicate with people. Don't be shy; many people love to say 'Hello', especially if they are going to be sat next to you for the next couple of hours on a train or coach. As long as you use your judgement when striking up a conversation and give the other person an opportunity to carry on with any reading or rest they had planned, you'll be amazed at the fascinating people you will meet. Just yesterday I said 'Hello' to a man waiting at the coach station and he shared that he was off to the British Museum to identify some moths that he had photographed recently. It turns out that he is one of the UK's leading authorities on the subject and responsible for the discovery of many previously unknown species. Apparently, there are over 2,000 species in the UK alone – amazing!

It also emerged that he is a school governor and interested in anything that will help with the employability of the young people in his school. I'd have thought networking skills might help, wouldn't you?

The bottom line when it comes to connecting is:

> *You do have to give a damn about other people. You've got to really be interested in what they're trying to achieve and want to help them if you can.*
>
> Andrew Horder, life coach and author of The Busy Fool

3 Meeting

Once you have connected, the relationship has started but it is definitely not off the ground yet. You need to follow up and meet up with your new friends as soon as possible to extend the friendship and see if there is anything you can do to help them. Sometimes you will have spotted something you can do when you first made a connection, like my meeting with the lepidopterist yesterday (you see, I did learn something), but quite often it takes a couple of meetings before you have a good idea as to what someone does so that you can make network connections for them.

Where you meet, is entirely up to you and your new friend. If you are meeting someone who is also unknown to your network, always suggest a fairly busy public space until you are completely comfortable. Generally, coffee shops, bars and business hubs are popular. Be sure to take with you anything that may add colour to the conversation, like the latest book you are reading or the business card of someone you think may be of interest to them. Don't take any sales literature or products, unless you have been specifically asked to do so. Let the conversation develop organically. If the topic of your products or services arises and they'd like to see something, then you have an excuse to meet up again or organize a web chat.

4 Listening

The best communicators are the best listeners and sometimes people just need a real good listening to! To generalize, a male brained person might be keen to solve the problem of the person they are listening to and want to jump in with a solution; whereas a female brained person is very comfortable adding their thoughts while the other person is still speaking. (To find out the sex of your brain, go to www.bbc.co.uk/science/humanbody/sex/add_user.shtml.) Both are missing a wonderful opportunity to get to know the other person and understand how they may be able to help them. To listen effectively, we have to park our own agenda and give the other person 100 per cent of our attention. This can be extremely difficult if you are a person with a busy mind because, as the other person is speaking, you might think of something that could help them and be tempted to interrupt. Don't do it though because you may miss something important. Instead, here's a tip I learned from my great friend Vanda North; if something the other person says sparks an idea in your mind, cross two fingers immediately. This simple anchoring technique will remind you what you were thinking when they stop talking and provide you with an opportunity to assess if it is still relevant when it is your turn to speak. It works a treat.

Remember to listen out for things that may be beneficial to them in all areas of their life not just their business or career needs. The purpose is to make a new friend and friends have an interest in the whole person.

5 Helping

> Giving connects two people, the giver and the receiver, and this connection gives birth to a new sense of belonging.
> Deepak Chopra, founder of the Chopra Center for Wellbeing, and New York Times *best-selling author*

In sales circles, people often talk of the law of reciprocation, but it just doesn't feel right to me. Effectively, the concept is that if I give someone a small gift they will feel emotionally compelled to give something in return, and that could include significant items such as the deposit for a car or a house! This is not the sort of premeditated concept that we are talking about when we are building a friendship. We're talking about selfless help; the sort of gesture that makes you feel just as good as they do and, as Deepak says, connects you both to each other. Help can come in many guises from advice, to a referral and through to financial assistance. The concept of giving first in a new relationship is firmly embedded into the philosophy of all major networking groups because it says that you value the other person and also demonstrates your commitment.

As your network grows, there will be certain people that are at the forefront of your mind by virtue of the value they bring into your life and it is generally these people that spring to mind when an opportunity or a valuable piece of information becomes available. Value can be measured in many ways and could simply be that they make you smile regularly, so be sure to pour your personality as well as your good heart into your networks regularly.

6 Supporting

Networking is about making friends and then keeping up to date with friends, catching up with friends. It's not really any different from when we first went to infant school, you know. I can still remember going to school for the first time, walking into the playground and being surrounded by people but we were all in the same boat. And so everybody made different friends and got involved with different groups, and I don't think it's any different in business or in work. It's about finding those people that you can get on with and that you can look out for each other. I don't think it's any more sophisticated or different than that.

Dave Clarke, CEO of NRG Business Networks

Our support network is the one made up of close relationships. How you define 'close' is up to you, but who do you turn to when the chips are down? Who provides the shoulder to cry on when life isn't going the way you hoped it would? Who is always there with that great piece of advice or emotional support when you need it? Think about how you relate to those people and how they interact with you generally. This is your model for building supportive relationships with the people in your networks. You won't necessarily form a close relationship with everyone in your network but it is important to develop some empathy. We haven't got time here to explore this in detail but there is a difference between sympathy and empathy, and the former is much less helpful to the individual than the latter. Sympathy is discovering someone in a hole in the ground and jumping right in there with them to join in the misery; empathy is recognizing they are in a challenging situation and reaching down to 'help them up'.

Before I finish with this idea of supporting people in your network, I want to share a story I heard once from a lady who was friends with someone who had just lost their husband. They were not close friends but when this lady spotted her friend on the high street, she stopped her, gave her a hug and said a few comforting words. Now, the sad thing about this story is that our subject was the first person to have done this, despite the fact that her friend was sure that she had seen several other friends that morning. Many people tend to avoid these situations, fearing that they will further upset their friend or perhaps even protecting themselves; but the reality is that, as human beings, we crave connection and any degree of support can only help if your intent is true, whether that be a hug, a phone call, an e-mail or a message via social media.

7 Trusting

Empathy and effective listening greatly assist the next step in our exploration of how to build relationships, building trust. These qualities require you to be genuinely interested in others; listening properly and reflecting back meaningfully and helpfully are great foundations for a new relationship. Following up, as we discussed earlier, is also a vital feature of building trust and reputation. However, trust is a multi-faceted thing and there are two additional qualities that we need to consider if we are to build trusting relationships.

The first is reliability. Who do you know that always does what they said they would do, keeps their commitments and never makes a commitment that they cannot keep? These are invaluable people to cultivate as strong relationships in your network. An individual who has a reputation for being both reliable and dependable is very easy to refer or recommend because the person doing the referring feels confident that their reputation is not at risk.

The second additional quality of a trusting relationship is integrity. In fact, integrity is the most commonly repeated quality that good networkers look for when developing their inner circle. You cannot have integrity 99 per cent of the time – it is an all-time thing. This doesn't mean that if someone makes a mistake that damages their personal integrity you can no longer trust them, but it does mean that if they fail to apologize for their wrong-doing and seek to redress the situation quickly, then there is some serious rebuilding to do within that relationship. This is because, failing to apologize for wrong-doing often damages a person's integrity and reputation far more than the original misjudgement itself. We only need to think of how we view politicians when they fail to take responsibility and admit their mistakes. Some integrity is lost. Do it a few times and all integrity is lost.

Put simply, integrity is vital for trust to develop and in networking terms, certain connections are absolutely impossible to make until a very high level of trust is established.

One final word on trust; you have probably heard of the phrase 'Trust is a two-way street' and recently, I had cause to stop and reflect on what that really means. I came across an individual who talked a lot about 'trust and faith' and how it was important for people to work with him in that way. However, it became quite evident that the same individual did not really have any trust and faith in the people that were working with him. Despite attracting some great people around him, his inability to work transparently and openly undermined every meaningful relationship. Think carefully about this one as it is an easy trap to fall into if you let bad life experiences colour your current reality. By all means exercise some caution but do not close your heart to the abundance of life.

8 Cheering

When was the last time you genuinely encouraged, praised or congratulated someone? This is equally important in both work and social settings.

If someone in your network has just run a marathon for charity, you can be sure that it has been an important part of their life for the past few months and that they are quite proud of their achievement. Why not cheer them on? Social media has made this so much easier than it used to be. You can now provide timely encouragement and feedback from anywhere in the world.

9 Asking

With all this talk of relationship building you could be forgiven for thinking that you should never ask for help from your network but, of course, that is

Social media provides an amazing opportunity to rebalance our communities. I am sure you will have recognized that there is very little 'good news' distributed by traditional media organizations. 'The News' is focused, almost entirely, on the things that are going wrong – disasters, scandals, corruption, crime and hatred. However, this traditional media does not reflect the sum total of our reality. There is far more good going on in people's lives and in our communities than is considered newsworthy, but that doesn't make it any less important to the individuals or communities concerned. The danger, from a networking perspective, is that we get drawn into this maelstrom of doom and gloom and cease to add value to our networks. Let me explain why…

If we give a proportionate amount of our attention to the good things that we see and hear then we will effectively be reinforcing the great behaviours of the individuals in our networks. Social media has come in for a lot of criticism from certain sectors of society for being banal and irrelevant, however, if you observe the behaviour on platforms such as Twitter, Facebook, Google+ and LinkedIn you will see countless examples of people helping people; people encouraging people and people cheering on people. As you would expect these supportive relationships are not confined by geography, culture, race, sex or religion. In fact just yesterday, I read the following: 'If the politicians, religious leaders, financiers and media would stay out of international affairs, we would find that most human beings are very happy to just get along with other human beings.' Personally, while I am not naïve enough to believe that the interests of the significant few are not powerful enough to maintain the status quo, I am pragmatic enough to realize the truth in the phrase that a stranger is a friend you haven't met yet. The potential for the overwhelming majority of good people to interact with their fellow human beings to build effective relationships and effective communities is amazing.

not the case. As long as you have proven your value to your network through exhibiting the sort of behaviours discussed above, then it is absolutely okay to ask for help when you need it; in fact, many people in your network would be upset if you didn't ask for help!

Do your best to ask in a way that respects the right for the other person to turn down your request if they are not completely comfortable either with you, or making the request of their network contacts. However, assuming they will be happy to help, brevity and clarity are critical. Make your request specific and actionable. We'll look at this in more detail in Chapter 10, Mobilizing your network.

10 Thanking

Saying thank you when a contact refers you is not just about good manners, it is also a great opportunity to further develop the relationship with the person who has kindly referred you.

Of course, one great way to 'say' thank you is by following up effectively with your new contact. Nothing demonstrates your appreciation as well as being a true professional. In the mind of your new contact, you are representing your mutual friend. You are a very real measure of the quality of their network, so do your best to get the basics right. Remember too to express how you personally feel about your mutual friend. The correct term for this is edification, which means simply saying good things about another person to boost their reputation. This is a selfless and generous thing to do and highlights your desire to be a great network connection.

Key points

> *Networking is always important when it's real, and it's always a useless distraction when it's fake.*
>
> Seth Godin, international best-selling author,
> entrepreneur, marketer, and public speaker

Networking is all about relationships. It's not about collecting followers, friends or business cards. It's about connecting with one individual at a time and creating mutual benefit.

Just how many connections you choose to make is the subject of our next chapter.

How big should my network be?

Count your garden by the flowers,

Never by the leaves that fall,

Count your days by golden hours,

Don't remember clouds at all;

Count your nights by stars, not shadows,

Count your life with smiles, not tears,

And with joy on this, your birthday,

Count your age by friends, not years.

Dixie Lee Crosby

I'm often asked, 'how big should my network be?'. However, the better question to ask is, 'what type of network should I build?'.

This is an important question to consider and, unlike the general agreement on 'what is networking', the experts that I interviewed, studied and listened to over the years are quite split on the type of network you should build. Some promote close referral networks and others advocate the opportunity to build expansive, almost unlimited, networks. So, what is the right answer? The answer is, it depends, but it is undoubtedly a critical question because your answer will determine how you spend your time building relationships. In this chapter we'll look at both arguments and propose a few questions you can ask yourself to decide what sort of network you want to build. Before we explore the options in more detail though, let's have a quick look at how our networks have grown throughout history.

The rise and rise of networks

As we mentioned in the previous chapter, we have been networking since the dawn of time, ever since we worked out that it made life easier to collaborate with our fellow hunters and gatherers. In the grand swathe of history, our networks have grown and grown as our understanding of the world has grown. The bigger the world became, the more people we met and the greater the need to form relationships to help us capitalize on the opportunities before us. Thus, a city dweller in the nineteenth century could easily have a network of several hundred people as they immersed themselves in the world of trade and commerce, whereas their predecessor from the fourteenth century could probably get by with a few dozen to ply their trade in their neighbourhood. In fact, it hasn't been a case of constant growth; the size of networks has ebbed and flowed as our knowledge and cultures have expanded and retracted. During the 100 or so years that preceded the introduction of the internet, networks generally stabilized and the concept of a manageable network took hold, with people citing Dunbar's Number of 150 as being the optimal number of people in your network as this was, they argued, a realistic number to actively manage (where 'managing' meant keeping in regular contact and developing great relationships). Certain individuals bucked the trend, cultivating expansive networks, but big networks were generally the preserve of specific careers rather than the norm; sales and politics being two areas that immediately spring to mind. In fact, there are many politicians, like George Bush Senior, who wrote a few letters each night to individuals in their networks to maintain the broad base of relationships they needed to stay connected and in power.

Going glocal

People talk a lot about the world shrinking as our ability to communicate globally has transformed our relationship building capacity. It is indubitably just as easy to have a conversation with someone the other side of the world as it is with our neighbour. In fact, some may argue it's easier because people are more available online than they are physically available to have a conversation over the fence! The advent of instant messaging and web chat on our mobile devices literally puts our global networks in our pocket. Interestingly, this has happened in the same timeframe as many of our geographically close networks have disintegrated. Mobility and commercial necessity has led many families to disperse, particularly in my lifetime. In the 1970s, the majority of families that I knew in my hometown of Barry in South Wales, were multi-generational, with children, parents, grandparents and great grandparents living within a few streets of each other. These days, this setup is rare. People travel further for work, for study and, ultimately, join new communities and they are supported every step of the way by speedier travel networks and technology. At the extreme, gone are the days that emigration meant an end to relationships. Webcams keep families and friends connected across the miles; albeit at the expense of physical intimacy, but the emerging virtual technology may even solve that problem too, soon!

The net result of all this is that, even at an organic level, we have bigger networks because as we move around and forge new relationships, technology enables us to simultaneously maintain older relationships.

We are truly members of a global community (even if we don't quite know how to do that very well at the moment), there are pioneers building glocal businesses and building relationships with people they've never actually physically met. This concept is not completely new of course. I remember having a penpal in the United States when I was a child. What is new though is the extent to which we can interact with our global family members. Just yesterday I was interviewing my new friend, Australian Keith Keller, over Skype to capture his expertise in all things related to Twitter and in the course of a short 60 minutes we were able to record the interview, exchange some documents and even make a couple of global referrals – not to mention discuss a few mutual connections!

What the experts say

As I indicated above, the experts are split on this one, so I thought I would present you with their key points and let you decide which approach suits you best.

Closed

The most traditional, and therefore most followed, path to networking is the closed one. Essentially, this view adheres to the notion that it is simply not possible to maintain a network of more than a couple of hundred people. Indeed, there is even a 'law' that some closed networkers cite to back up their approach – Dunbar's Law. This often cited law states that our brains lack the capacity to maintain and nurture more than 150 relationships at a time, thereby diminishing the ability of groups larger than this to form and thrive. Of course, from a networking perspective, our 150 contacts may not need to thrive as a group, we may be very happy for most of them to be totally ignorant of the existence of the rest. However, many closed networks have proven that there is additional benefit in everyone getting to know everyone else really well, especially when it comes to unearthing opportunities for each other.

There are other benefits to closed networks, not least of which is a sense of community and identity when the group puts the work in to get to know each other. The psychological benefits of feeling like you belong to a group are significant and make it easier to relax and even look forward to meeting up. Then there is the very visible benefit exchange that goes on in closed networks; often the group will see when members are helping each other, further enhancing the perspective of the relationships across the whole group. Finally, it is worth noting the efficiency of closed networks. For example, if you need a solicitor to help you sell your house and there is one in your BNI group, you don't need to search anywhere else. BNI – Business Network International – is the world's largest offline business networking group and through their membership of the group, the solicitor will have established their credibility already and so all the hard work is done for you.

Another example of a closed network is the hugely beneficial Mastermind Group. Usually made up of a diverse group of members with varied life experiences and outside networks, a Mastermind Group comes together to support each other, solve problems and generate ideas to move the whole group forward. An environment of high trust is essential.

The potential drawback of closed networks is the limitation they put on learning and opportunities. Studies have shown that when a group of friends or a family have been together for a long time, their knowledge overlaps substantially as they share what they know. Only the introduction of new members or outside expertise can expand the thinking or indeed, the awareness of new opportunities.

Selective

A selective networker is a type of closed networker. Essentially, they are asking themselves a question when a potential new connection arrives: 'Do I want this person in my network?' They will ignore the standard formatted LinkedIn requests and even more personalized requests are scrutinized for both accuracy and potential (however they measure that – usually in short-term tactical terms). Their aim is to build a network that they can vouch for, if asked. This makes sense from an efficiency perspective because it means they don't have to stop and think when a connection request is made within their network. It also means that they can keep up with everything that is going on inside their network, through the online timelines and at offline meetings.

Like their closed networker friends, what selective networkers miss out on though are the more random opportunities and overall general effectiveness of an open networking approach. By questioning the value of an individual, they are dismissing the opportunity that lies within that person's network or even within that individual's future. As I mentioned earlier, I could have never known the value that some people in my network would be to me in putting this book together when I met them (some more than 30 years ago). Some would argue that they are happy to launch a campaign when they want to access a certain organization or individual, but this is a bit like digging your well when you are thirsty. Personally, I think this approach to networking is based on the most frequent warning of childhood – don't talk to strangers. Selective networkers are happy to talk to people they know, or to personal recommendations from within their networks, but they are rarely proactive or responsive to unknowns!

Open

The term open networker is quite a recent one; in fact it seems to be synonymous with LinkedIn, although there are obviously other platforms that make it easy to connect with people you don't know, such as Twitter and Pinterest. A LinkedIn Open Networker (or LION) is someone who has added their name to a list of other open networkers or joined groups focused entirely on making connections.

Open networking does come at a price; you have to work out how to manage potentially large numbers of e-mails, connection requests, irrelevant news items and spam. This translates as more things on your daily to-do list, but there are pluses that may make this organizing task worth the price to you.

First, diversity; if you only connect to people you already know, you are limiting your potential exposure to the richness of the global community. The alternative is a bit like turning up to a networking event and only talking to your friends. The idea of networking is to build relationships and you can't do that unless you interact with people. Your opportunity to learn from this diverse network is incredible too. Reaching out to new groups explodes the potential knowledge of all involved.

Second, is the opportunity to improve the odds of building an exceptional network. Thomas Power, online networking expert, has suggested that you probably want an inner circle (your closest network) of about 50 people. If your current inner circle does not include some of the people (or, more accurately, types of people) that you would love to have there, then what strategy do you have in mind for meeting them? Open networking can get you closer to the people you would like to meet, quicker. This happened for me a few years back when I was running an innovation project for a client. The client decided that they would like to visit a number of innovative businesses to expose themselves to the cultures and new ideas; one hour later, I had made contact with individuals in 15 of their list of top 20 targets and we ended up being able to visit eight of the businesses within the next month. Most of them were second level connections in my network and I had a variety of people I could ask to make the introduction.

Finally, ask yourself, are you generally an open-hearted person? Are you the sort of person who is happy to chat to someone you may meet on a train or in a bookstore? Would you be excited to welcome a new relative into the family? If you answered either of these questions in the affirmative, then open networking will mirror your usual approach to life. Essentially, an open networker is not evaluating the value of the individual in front of them and deciding if they want to connect, they are connecting anyway on the assumption that there will almost certainly be some value they can add to the life of the other, or vice versa. There is strategic value in this approach too; most opportunities in life do not come from your close networks but from your distant and weakest ties and it's the same online. I have made some fantastic connections and learned an incredible amount via my connections on LinkedIn – some of whom I had never actually conversed with previously.

Hybrid

Hybrid networkers seek to get the best from the other approaches. They are proactive, effective, have an open and expansive view of the world and yet also develop incredibly efficient ways to deal with large networks and exchange maximum value with their network connections.

At the 'open' end of the networking spectrum, they happily consider all connection requests, will make connections within their network (even if they don't know both parties intimately) and reach out to new groups and individuals to share knowledge and provide support.

At the 'closed' end of the networking spectrum, hybrid networkers are happy to join selective groups and always have an inner circle of trusted individuals. They are also open to the idea of identifying key influencers in outside networks to access new areas and relationships for mutual development and growth.

My experience is that the group of people who are my close friends is constantly changing. Some, a few, will be there for a lifetime, many will be there for years, but some will join that inner circle, stay for a short while and leave, either because we find, as we deepen the relationship, that we are actually not of a like mind, or because other circumstances intervene.

Looking back, my guess is that my inner circle half-life is about ten years. In other words, every ten years around 75 people that I know well, trust, respect, work closely with, drop out of my inner circle of close friends. But they're replaced with an equal number of new people whose relationships are deepening.

William Buist, collaboration specialist, director at Abelard Management Services Limited

Very few open networkers keep in touch with the thousands of people in their networks. The timelines and inboxes on LinkedIn allow you to maintain an awareness of the activities within your network, but as the numbers continue to grow, these become less and less effective. However, through smart utilization of the Search functionality and a willingness to engage in random conversations on occasion, it is possible to have an enlarged group of network contacts who are more than just faces and numbers. Moreover, if you are willing to provide good content through the social media components of these networking sites, then you will be a more prominent member in the networks of your network.

The argument for open networking

I think the key indicator for wealth is not good grades, work ethic, or IQ. I believe it's relationships. Ask yourself two questions: How many people do I know, and how much ransom money could I get for each one?
Jarod Kintz, author of E-mails from a Madman

As you have probably gathered by now, I am an advocate for open networking, particularly on LinkedIn. In my last book, *Mastering Time*, I shared the following list of benefits that I have derived from adopting an open networking approach:

- Old friends have been able to reconnect with me because they saw me as a link in their friends' networks.

- Opportunities have found me as my knowledge and expertise spread through blogs and answering others' questions.

- My ability to help others and make a difference has increased exponentially as I share my time with thousands rather than individuals.

- My opportunities to learn have been enhanced. Acquaintances, and indeed, random connections, by definition, know people that we do not, and thus are able to share more novel information.

- The quality of some of my closest business relationships has improved. I have worked with some great people, but I know that there are always people with more knowledge, better solutions and quicker delivery capabilities that are going to be the pioneers of the future. I will never meet them if I adopt a closed approach to networking. I may never meet them if I adopt an open approach, but it is no more time consuming and infinitely more time efficient to try.

I've made new friends. It was the title of my good friend Thomas Power's first book, *A Friend In Every City* that first attracted me to online networking. Having watched him build his businesses online for the past 15 years, I can verify that this is not idealism. However, I've heard some of my own friends say, in explanation of why they do not network online, that they have all the friends they want and don't need new friends. Some of these friends are people I have only met in the last few years, so I wonder if they are truly that discerning! When it comes to community, relationships and love, the road less travelled is a lonely road.

How your network grows

If you are sitting there reading this and wondering how on earth you are going to develop a network of 150 people, don't panic! You're probably already further along than you think. If we think of networks growing out from us at their centre, like the diagram below, then the numbers soon build up. Why don't you grab a piece of paper and a pen or open a drawing App and follow along with me?

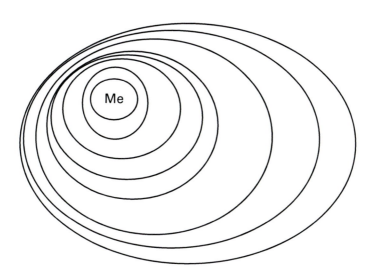

Start with a small circle in the centre of the page and write your initials inside. Then draw another circle just outside it and write the names of your immediate family inside that circle. Next, draw another slightly larger circle; this time add the names of your extended family, or if you are like me with a huge family, just write down the number of cousins, aunts and uncles, second cousins, in-laws and outlaws that you have. Keep drawing larger circles, each time populating them with numbers to reflect who you know; label each circle so that you can recall the groups later. This list of groups may help you build your picture:

- close friends;
- childhood friends;
- school friends;
- teachers;
- family friends;
- college/university friends;
- girlfriends/boyfriends;
- lecturers;
- casual job colleagues;
- friends made on holidays;
- first job colleagues;
- subsequent jobs colleagues;
- current colleagues;
- suppliers;
- clients;
- neighbours old and new;
- clubs and associations;
- hobbies;
- fellow parents;
- acquaintances; and
- service providers.

You may feel like it is a bit strange to include the people you know in some of these categories because you haven't seen them for years, but just imagine what would happen if you bumped into them on the street or online tomorrow, how would the conversation go? It is very likely that, even if you were not really close friends previously, you would have many things to chat about and many common threads; certainly a lot more than some of the new relationships that you have developed.

I'm not advocating that you maintain such a diagram, adding new relationships as you form them, but this rigorous approach to capturing your network will hopefully demonstrate to you just how big your existing network is and how it will continue to grow in the years ahead.

Fit for purpose

So, where does this leave us with regard to selecting an appropriate personal networking approach? Let's start with the smallest number our experts would recommend you look to bring into your network – Dunbar's 150 people. Closed networkers maintain that 150 is a significant number of people to have in your network at any one time, so if your network is smaller than this, then you now have a target. 150 people in the whole world, that's 1 person in every 46 million. Look around you: would you say that your network is the best it could be to meet your personal aspirations? If not, then it's time to decide how you are going to supplement it.

Apart from the emotional reasons that some people choose closed approaches and some choose more open approaches to networking, there are a few tactical questions you may want to ask as you decide on your approach:

1   Will you or your business benefit from a strong local network? If so, a selective, referral-based, network will work best for you.
2   Is the market for you or your business regional or national? If so, open regional events and online networks will be a good combination.
3   Is your market international or global? If so, groups with international ties would be worth joining, supported by selective connecting online and, if you want to take the long-term view, supplemented by an open strategy.

Tessa Hood summed it up neatly:

> *Have you chosen the most appropriate group to join? Look carefully at the members of a network and ensure that you're not wasting your time. Small local groups may be fine if you are a florist, cake-maker, solicitor, plumber, accountant, estate agent, or local health club, but if your market (or job) is in multi-national organizations, City businesses, or similar, ensure that you are networking with the right peer group. You can waste an awful lot of time trying to develop relationships with small organizations, when you (or your business) are completely outside their sphere.*
>
> Tessa Hood, Personal Brand and Reputation
> Developer and author of The Personal
> Brandwagon (…and how to jump on it)

Notice, Tessa is not saying that the people in the local network might be a waste of your time, because they may certainly have links to people in your target markets; it's just that, if you are an international consultant, what you do may not result in many referrals for you from a local network and, more importantly, you may have less to offer such a group in terms of usable referrals either. You need to find a group that would welcome an opportunity to talk to your contacts so that you can provide lots of value straight away.

You may find it helpful to also think in terms of networks rather than just one big network. Here are some good examples of networks you may want to consider.

Your career network

Your reasons for networking may not revolve around business today, but as you start to think about networking in general, you may wish to consider the fact that, according to the latest figures, the average number of jobs a person will have in their career is now more than 11. Job searching and networking have become an integral part of everyday work life, rather than something you do once or twice during your career. Do you know where your next job or career step will take you? Are your networks diverse enough to provide you with choices?

Steadily building your networks over time will serve you well when it comes to learning more about your dream job or career. If you work in an office currently and have always fancied running your own bar, it makes sense to find out more about that line of work, and what better way to do that than to ask some people that are doing it already? You can return the favour and relieve them of some of their stock in the process – perfect!

Diversity within your networks is extremely helpful when it comes to landing that next job. As I mentioned already, no-one can know exactly what is ahead of them in life and so only building networks in your current industry, can leave you a bit exposed if there is a downturn in your sector. By all means, build quality relationships in your field, but make sure you're constantly adding to your wider network – think of it as a sort of long-term insurance. However, make sure that you are forming these other relationships with mutual benefit in mind and always be on the lookout for ways to help your connections.

Finally, keeping in touch with former colleagues is easier today than it has ever been. Depending on the sort of relationship you have with them, you are probably linked to them through Facebook, Google+ or LinkedIn, or possibly even all three. As a minimum, take an interest in their journey and, as they switch jobs, change career direction or get promoted, be sure to congratulate them. It's easy, it keeps the relationship alive and it doesn't have to be in any way motivated by your personal agenda. In fact, as your network grows, you may find that you can help them at these points of transition by introducing them to some relevant and valuable connections.

Your support network

Who supports you as you travel through life? Who do you support? There are times in life when everything is not running as smoothly as we would like or when we could really do with some help. New joiners to the workforce are the obvious example of a group in society that benefit greatly from having around them a group of people that can offer some time, some financial support or even just a listening ear. Typically, this network will be made up of family and close friends, but often, it's the second tier networks of your support network that identify job openings and work experience opportunities.

At the other end of the timeline, you may find that, as you get older, your desire to remain independent could be reinforced from knowing that there is a group of people you can depend upon to be there for you.

The social network

This is the network that most people develop without knowing it. We naturally gravitate towards people that share our values, our interests, our passions, our aspirations, our desires and our sense of humour. We know that we will have fun with this group of people and so we choose to spend time with them. However, it doesn't hurt to think about this group as a specific network as you get older and life becomes more hectic, because it is incredibly easy to lose touch and not see or hear from them, from one year to the next. Usually, this does not affect the strength of the underlying friendship when you do meet up, but it can feel like time wasted if you always have a great time and you don't make time for them (and yourself) in between. As with all networks, invest just a bit of time as often as you can. Otherwise, your time will get swallowed up with your other networks.

Your community network

Your community network is often the easiest to overlook. Increasingly, we live in streets and communities in which we do not even know our neighbours. Work may take us out of the house early in the morning, and when we return home there may be little time for anything other than food, washing, chatting to close friends and family, and sleep. Relationships may emerge, if there are children involved, as you participate in school and club related activities and bump into other parents; and similarly, your own pastimes may introduce you to others who share your interests. Nevertheless, the overriding trend is towards groups of people who share public amenities, pavements and street lighting but are almost completely oblivious to the lives of their neighbours! It doesn't have to be that way and you can change it if that is a fair description of your current situation. Introduce yourself to your neighbours, get involved in local community groups (even if they are child related initially) and generally create a community around you! Think about the benefits:

- You'll feel more secure in your own home.
- You will have boosted your support network.
- You'll meet some great new friends who already share your taste in locations.
- Your sense of personal self-esteem will be boosted as you make a tangible difference to the people around you.

Of course, these days we live in much bigger communities if you take into account the ones online too. By joining social networks online we have the ability to interact with people from across the world at the touch of a button. For those with limited mobility, this can be a great source of comfort as they use tools such as Skype and Google Hangouts to stay connected.

Key points

It is our choices, Harry, that show what we truly are, far more than our abilities.

J K Rowling, Harry Potter and the Chamber of Secrets

- The size of your network is a choice, based on your approach to life and the level of your desire to interact with your fellow human beings.
- In the next chapter, we'll dig deeper and explore your networking style.

What's your networking style?

Style is a simple way of saying complicated things.
Jean Cocteau, poet, novelist, dramatist, designer,
playwright, artist and filmmaker

When it comes to building relationships, the first thing you will encounter is complexity. As human beings, most of us are capable of displaying behaviour at opposite ends of any spectrum we choose to use, within seconds. Most people can switch from joy to sadness, from ecstasy to depression and from the minutiae to the big picture with little difficulty. Consequently, when you are networking with others, it is possible to feel as if you are always 'on the back foot' when it comes to making a connection. That vivacious individual you were laughing with almost incessantly last time you met, has suddenly become fixated on the details of a proposition you are making; or that friendly, relaxed individual you were having a very amiable cup of coffee with just last week, is now almost too busy to even smile. What's going on? More importantly, how do you build a relationship with these chameleons? The answer lies in an understanding of networking styles.

What's your networking style?

I was first introduced to the idea that we should deal with different people differently through the hilarious presentations of Dr Robert Rohm. Until that time, I thought I was a genius for working out that it was perhaps a

Ever since Hippocrates, the Ancient Greek philosopher and medical doctor, identified that his patients behaved in four quite different and distinctive ways, the human race has sought to understand what it is that makes an individual act the way they do. Aristotle linked the same four elements to Earth, Air, Fire and Water and more recently, the psychologist Carl Jung began to talk of 'preferences' rather than fixed traits. Today, there are many psychometric profiling tools that can dissect your every attribute but I have found that the simplified Jungian model is not only the easiest to understand but also the most intuitive to put into action. Jung talked about four opposite pairs of preferences:

- Introverted and extroverted.
- Intuitive and sensing.
- Thinking and feeling.
- Judging and perceiving.

The simplified model that I use to help people understand differences quickly, utilizes Jung's preferences and aligns them with colour to make them memorable. I like to use the word 'style' as it reminds you to reflect on how the behavioural preferences of others impacts on the way we perceive them.

good idea to try to 'relate' to others, and that the quickest way to do that was to be 'more like them' when I was with them. Little did I know that my desire to get along with people, rather than being a reflection of some amazing intelligence, was merely an indicator of my personal style.

What follows are exaggerated descriptions of the four styles; however, as you will see later, every individual has a unique mix of these styles and is very able to raise their energy in any style they choose to get a job done. The purpose of the descriptions that follow are to provide the extremes of the behaviour you will see so that you can practise observing these styles in action. All four of our characters have been invited to the same conference.

Richard Red

Richard decided that he would aim to arrive just before the main speaker was due on stage, thereby skipping the formalities and introductions. He

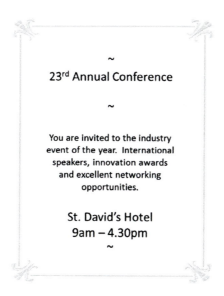

~

23rd Annual Conference

~

You are invited to the industry
event of the year. International
speakers, innovation awards
and excellent networking
opportunities.

St. David's Hotel
9am – 4.30pm
~

asked a good friend (Yasmin Yellow) to save him a seat and consequently, when he arrived, he spotted her immediately and headed straight for her row to take his seat. They greeted enthusiastically and settled down for the main speaker. Of course, there were some important pieces of business he needed to attend to via his blackberry, and he needed to excuse himself just before the end of the talk to take an urgent call, but otherwise, he was very attentive and thoroughly enjoyed the talk. Thankfully, it was a speaker who got straight down to business and didn't obscure his message with lots of flowery examples.

During the first break, Richard enjoyed a drink with Yasmin and thanked her for helping him earlier. Just then he spotted the main conference organizer who he had been meaning to meet for a while. Richard headed straight over and introduced himself, confidently and directly: 'Hi, I'm Richard Red, it's great to meet you. I appreciate you're very busy now, but could you spare three minutes later, I've got a proposition I want to run by you that I know you're going to like. Literally three minutes…'

The organizer was a bit taken aback but agreed to meet Richard at the end of the day. And so it continued… by 5 pm, Richard had managed to speak to all six of his targets and set up three appointments. One of Richard's favourite mottos is **'The bottom line is, he who dares wins'** and so he was feeling great by the time he headed back to the hotel.

Yasmin Yellow

Yasmin whooped with delight when she received her invitation. There's absolutely nothing better than spending a day with all of the movers and shakers in the industry, she thought, and the hotel chosen for this year's conference is always fabulous.

On the day of the conference, Yasmin arrived about five minutes after most people were in and drinking their coffees and she noisily greeted the first group she encountered. Everyone loves Yasmin's infectious enthusiasm and her obvious love of people. People were calling her over from all parts of the foyer and consequently, she ended up quite near the front of the queue, heading into the main hall, for the start of the conference. She sat right in the middle of Row 3 and put her bag down to reserve a seat for her good friend Richard who would be arriving a bit later. She was still talking and greeting people as the hosts took the stage, her excitement was fairly bubbling over, with a smile from ear to ear. The only things brighter than her smile were her clothes which helped her stand out from the very large crowd that had assembled for the conference. A little while later, her good friend Richard arrived. They hadn't seen each other for more than 36 hours, so they were long overdue a big hug. 'Isn't life great,' she thought!

Most people in her circle admire Yasmin's effortless networking. She seems to just get on with everyone and always has something good to say about the people in her life. She is also great at helping people connect and introducing people to each other. The phrase, **Give people an introduction to live up to,** is one she has never forgotten. Yasmin has an ability to have fun wherever she goes and this is hugely attractive, even to people that have not met her yet. There is nothing as attractive as someone who is obviously having fun and Yasmin's sunny disposition disarms any reservations people may have about introducing themselves.

Yasmin's network have a knack of ensuring that she meets just the right person and throughout the day, she was introduced to a few individuals that she had been hoping to meet for some time. As she headed for the bar at the hotel later, she told one of these new contacts: 'I have the best, most loyal and wonderful friends in the world and I'm very glad to have you join them!'

Gulab Green

Gulab was quietly pleased to have been invited to the conference and set about contacting a few of her closest colleagues to find out who else was going and, in the process, ended up organizing the car sharing arrangements.

When she arrived at the conference, she bumped into an old friend who was on the reception team and as they chatted, Gulab realized that her friend could probably do with some help directing people into the hall. It also gave them more time to catch up. She was still on the door when Richard Red turned up. Gulab suggested that he take a vacant seat near the back because the event had filled up from the front and those were the next seats available. However, Richard had spotted Yasmin Yellow near the front of the audience and was already heading that way. As he speeded off, Gulab's only thought was for all of the people in the row that now had to stand up and let him through.

During the breaks at the conference, Gulab spent most of her time with the people she knew but did enjoy the opportunities to engage with other people that joined the group and always seemed to be focused on helping them get the best from the day. Her quiet, calm approach made everyone around her feel comfortable and she ended up having a couple of great conversations over coffee. Two conversations in particular made the whole day worthwhile. One was with the friend she had helped on the door earlier in the day – she had a fantastic project for Gulab to consider. The second was with a friend of a friend who had just obtained the licence to import the very item that her husband had been looking for to expand his business. As she relaxed in the bar later, Gulab reflected that neither opportunity could have been foreseen at the start of the day, but, as she always says, 'It's amazing what happens *when you're just making friends.*'

Bill Blue

Bill was keen to arrive at the conference early because the invitation hadn't been clear as to when the very first session started. He checked his coat into the cloakroom, requested a cup of Earl Grey tea and studied the agenda. Occasionally, he looked up to see who else was arriving but when they opened the doors to the main hall, he joined the queue and ended up on the end of the third row – perfect for getting in and out quickly during the breaks.

He struck up a conversation with the gentleman next to him and they were both amused to find that they shared the same initials and owned the same make of car. This had been discovered when Bill spotted that his neighbour had a keyring with the initials WRB on it. Bill's full name was William Robert Blue or Billy Bob as he was called, rather embarrassingly, as a child. They laughed at this small disclosure and, with the ice broken, proceeded to have a great conversation about the day ahead.

Half an hour later, as the audience waited for the main speaker to take the stage, Bill was a little irritated to be asked to stand up by someone who was quite clearly arriving late and yet heading for a prime seat in the middle of the row! However, as the person was preparing to take their seat, Bill recognized it was his old friend Richard Red and the two exchanged a smile as Bill mockingly pointed at his watch.

Throughout the rest of the day, Bill and his neighbour (Wade Buckley) got to know each other quite well, sharing stories of the challenges they were having managing the dependencies within their current projects. After the last speaker had left the stage, they formally exchanged business cards and said goodbye. **Slow but steady,** he thought. However, on one level, Bill was feeling a bit disappointed with himself for not 'networking' and meeting lots of people as the rest of the crowd appeared to have done. He'd attended several of these conferences now and each time promised himself (and his boss) that he would make more effort.

As he headed for the cloakroom to collect his coat though, something quite brilliant happened. Wade tapped him on the shoulder and insisted Bill follow him across the foyer to meet some people he had just met. It turns out that among the group was someone who Wade thought might be able to help Bill with his current project. In fact, it was better than that because the individual had actually faced the very same problem just recently and so had first-hand and recent experience of how to overcome the problem. Perfect. Bill's boss would be extremely happy!

The styles at a glance

The illustration on page 37 provides a snapshot of each style, the key aspects that will reveal themselves through the behaviour of the people you interact with when they are at their most relaxed and acting instinctively – or as Jung would have phrased it, acting according to their preferences.

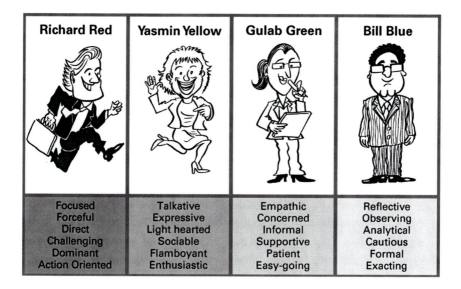

Richard Red	Yasmin Yellow	Gulab Green	Bill Blue
Focused	Talkative	Empathic	Reflective
Forceful	Expressive	Concerned	Observing
Direct	Light hearted	Informal	Analytical
Challenging	Sociable	Supportive	Cautious
Dominant	Flamboyant	Patient	Formal
Action Oriented	Enthusiastic	Easy-going	Exacting

So, armed with this information, which style best reflects you on a good day? How do you tend to behave? Put the four styles in order, where the number 1 (your primary style) is how you prefer to act, followed by your secondary and tertiary styles. Finally, you are left with your lowest preference.

How the styles work

However, just when you thought that you may have discovered the key to this relationship puzzle, the lines start to become indistinct and the edges blurred. As I implied previously, nobody is 100 per cent red, or yellow, or green or blue, *all of the time*. We are all a unique combination of the styles and more than capable of raising the energy of any one of the four styles when necessary. For example, if your style preference is massively yellow, you will still be able to complete a detailed government form – it just may not be that much fun for you and completing it may not fill you with a huge sense of achievement (more like a massive sense of relief).

Indeed, to provide a real example, as I am writing this book I am constantly concerned that I will forget something important to you the reader and have therefore created, quite detailed, mind maps for each chapter (my naturally green style being supported by my not so natural but competent blue energy).

The good news about this though is that we all have the ability to relate to others, simply by adjusting our energy to match theirs. We don't have to be someone we are not, we just need to tap into our own version of the style being displayed by the people we encounter, to instantly relate and make it easier for them to connect with us.

Our secondary style is also important, especially if it is relatively close to our primary style. When your preference for your first and second styles is similar, it opens up a much broader spectrum of opportunity for you in terms of relating to others. Conversely, if our primary style is really strong, then we may experience instant rapport with some and take an almost instant dislike to others. Our least preferred style usually indicates the behaviour which we would find most challenging in others; although, Dr Robert Rohm used to talk about the attractiveness of opposites too. Very often, people find themselves in work or personal partnerships with individuals who balance their style with an opposite set of preferences. On a practical level, these relationships are not always easy though, because our natural style dictates the way we communicate and the barriers this creates, while sometimes humorous, can be frustrating for all involved.

Hopefully, if you have gathered anything from this chapter so far, it is that, very little of this is about you. Does it really matter if your style is predominantly red when you enter a room full of people with lots of green energy? Absolutely not: you now have the knowledge to raise your green energy, share a few friendly anecdotes, relax a bit, loosen your tie and just generally tune into the much gentler pace of your new friends. This is powerful stuff and, if you think about it, has within it the seeds of something that could transform relationships not just in our own community, but across the world. Red energy is red energy, wherever it is displayed. I have worked with global teams which have suddenly realized that the old adage 'there is more that unifies us than divides us' suddenly springs to life for them. These colour energies – our styles, are consistent regardless of religion, ethnicity or gender. Our ability to raise our energy to connect with the styles around us is our passport to the global community.

Recognizing the styles online

Having presented you with our four characters in an offline situation, you are now well on your way to being able to recognize the styles in action, but is it just as easy online? You'll be pleased to hear that the answer is 'Yes', *if* you remember to look at the style not the individual. Some people behave a little differently online than they do when you meet them face-to-face. This may not be intentional, it could just be environmental. Many people interact online when they are either in transit, and so preferring to be brief, or when they are sat in the comfort of their home and therefore able to be more eloquent, relaxed or witty. Sometimes the disconnected nature of the internet has the exact opposite effect too, affording people a sense of security in a debate or less cordial interaction. From your perspective, just deal with the style you perceive and focus always on the relationship.

So, let's have a look at some examples of the styles online. Again, I'll utilize our four characters to illustrate the style in as pure a way as possible; all you need to do is just focus on the style being presented.

Richard Red online

Richard often wondered in one of his self-styled 'rapid reflection' moments, what value he was actually getting out of all this social media. 'What is the bottom line?' was his favourite question whenever he met a real enthusiast. It was an honest question. Richard genuinely liked the speed with which he could raise something and get it out to his 'followers', so if someone could just quantify the benefits he would happily just get on with it.

As yellow was Richard's secondary style preference, the main place he interacts online is Facebook. He likes the way he can make a splash, throw up a few photos and generally broadcast a few simple messages instantly. His brother, equally red but with a strong blue secondary style, prefers the structure and more corporate feel of LinkedIn. Richard's style online is immediately obvious. His short punchy statements, questions or even random ideas are the epitome of brevity:

💬 'Who knows what's happening on Wall St?'

💬 'Heading to London, who's around?'

💬 'This is nonsense.'

💬 'Where have all the bananas gone?'

Some people interpret Richard's red style as brusque, but he would say it is 'to the point'. If there is a debate on a social business networking site like SunZu, his contribution will be succinct, opinionated and written as if what he is stating are facts. It's for others to worry about the details and to pick holes in the logic. By the time they have mulled it over, Richard Red has moved on to six other topics. It's not that he doesn't wish to engage in debate, it's more that he feels life is too short.

Yasmin Yellow online

Yasmin loves networking online. It's another myriad of opportunities to chat, share ideas and generally be her sunny self. There's no real method to her online networking, she's just happy interacting with her friends and loves the fact that she can reconnect with people and deal with certain aspects of her life in a flash. For example, her best friend and neighbour from a few years ago got in touch with her yesterday and it reminded her that she'd been out of touch with a number of friends since she had moved house (two moves ago). Within an hour, Yasmin had reconnected with six great friends, organized a trip and even started a conversation that looked like it might lead to some work.

Yasmin's style online, as you would imagine, is highly engaging and filled with colour. Lots of 'smileys', plenty of superfluous exclamation marks and an abundance of kisses. These are as natural to Yasmin as falling off a log. Why wouldn't you share the love? Finally, when someone's yellow energy is overflowing, it is always accompanied by long messages; why use one word when you can use 24?

Here's an example of one of Yasmin's recent interactions (disguising the names of the organizations for obvious reason!):

Hellooooo Peter! Please forgive the lack of communication over the last couple of weeks, it's been incredibly hectic here – in a good way though. I've been fielding calls from the CEO's of Grumbles plc and Sniffle Group, as well as coaching execs from Junipers, Thistles and Parsleys.

How's it all going at your end? I bet you're loving your new job! Well, Sweetness, keep smiling and I look forward to our monthly soirée next Monday night!!!

Luv 'n' Hugs, Yazza xxxxxx

It would be very easy, and a big mistake, to misinterpret Yasmin Yellow's style and assume that it is all fluff. Nothing could be further from the truth. A lifetime of interacting with people, building awesome relationships and engaging others effortlessly, means that she has a lot of knowledge, insights and skills that have eluded most people. Her contributions to online discussions are often filled with dynamic thinking, expansive ideas and always... quite long!

Gulab Green online

Like Yasmin, Gulab Green loves meeting her friends online and is a big user of Facebook. Her style is quite different to Yasmin though, less dramatic and more considered. Being very people oriented, and sensitive to emotive writing, Gulab loves to post inspiring pictures and quotes. Her heart is of pure intent, she's just hoping that someone out there will have their spirit lifted as a result of her latest update. On LinkedIn, Gulab enjoys tracking down people from her past and reconnecting. She has a great memory for the little things in life and this makes her a great connector too. Often, she will intuitively know where the great referral opportunities are in her network and make an introduction that surprises and delights both parties. In some ways, you could easily miss Gulab online, among all the noise created by the Yasmin Yellows and Richard Reds, but she quietly goes about her business; 'liking' an update here or making a brief 'comment' there – invariably uplifting and sometimes with cheeky, soft humour. Here are some recent examples:

- 'Congratulations on the new job Jim, that's great news! No more lazing about in bed till noon.'

- 'Thought you might like to see this short video, what an inspiration for all of us.'

- 'Saturday night in with my favourite girls, my favourite man and my favourite wine!!!'

This last update reminds me of another big part of Gulab Green's online persona; her family and friends mean a lot to her and, not surprisingly, her timeline will be filled with anecdotes, quips and pictures of her nearest and dearest. How much of this you see will depend on her level of concern over privacy and security, but you won't miss the sentimentality.

Bill Blue online

Being slightly more introverted than our other characters, Bill Blue absolutely loves networking online. He is able to add lots of value, make connections and generally demonstrate his expertise, all from the comfort of his own home. As we found earlier, live events with lots of people are not Bill's natural habitat, but a one-to-one meeting or a Skype chat are perfect, not to mention the efficiency gains!

LinkedIn particularly pleases Bill, with its structure, its focus on facts rather than conversation and the built-in processes for engagement, he couldn't ask for anything more (except perhaps a time monitor so that he could self-manage his time online)!

Bill's style is relatively formal online. He has a wicked sense of humour, but it is usually quite dry and he wouldn't want to risk a relationship for the sake of a quick joke. Of course, he has studied the platform and knows how to utilize it for maximum effectiveness. He's probably written a book about LinkedIn, or at least a quick start guide for the people in his close network. When looking for people with the same energy as Bill online, look for numbers, factual references, links and the most comprehensive referrals. Also, look for language like:

Dear George,

Thank you for the opportunity to meet and get to know each other yesterday. I trust you had a good journey back. As promised, here is an introduction to Sarah Gold who is a successful health analyst and involved in 6 projects across 4 counties. I am positive you will find mutual benefit in connecting. Do not hesitate to contact me if I can help you Link with anyone else.

Kind regards, Bill Blue.

As with most things, Bill's style online is to under promise and over deliver. So he won't say that he'll get you that link you need by lunchtime, he'll prepare you for the fact that it might be a week before he will have the time to help and then do it all with extreme grace within three days.

Networking using styles

So, how do we pull it all together? How do we utilize our understanding of the four styles when we are networking? The secret, as I'm sure you will have gathered already, is to be flexible and know that you have the ability to raise the relevant energy in you at any time to connect with any of the styles as you engage with people. To follow our extreme examples, if Simon or I knew all four of our characters and were to meet them at the same event, *and they were behaving according to their normal style*, we would exchange a vigorous handshake with Richard Red, a huge hug and noisy kisses with Yasmin, a lovely warm hug with Gulab and a formal 'How do you do?' with Bill. All of which would make them feel comfortable and at ease immediately.

Remember, this is not about you. What we're interested in here is building great relationships, so doesn't it make sense to engage with our network in ways that make it easier for them to relate to us? I know that many of you will be worried that relating to styles in this way may be perceived as manipulative at worst and inauthentic at best, but the reality is, your preferred style will always shine through once you are comfortable and your network contact is comfortable. Over time, what happens is the *relationship* develops its own rhythm, which is a hybrid of your combined styles. For example, if your preferred style is green and your best friend has a dominant red preference, the likelihood is your conversations will be louder and more energetic than your usual and more focused on quirky human behaviour than they would usually entertain. The key is to be yourself, but be a more expansive, flexible version of yourself.

Key points

Be who you are and say what you feel, because those who mind don't matter and those who matter don't mind.'
Theodor Seuss Geisel (Dr Seuss), writer, poet, and cartoonist

- Be true to yourself, act with authenticity and your natural networking style will attract your perfect network.

- Let's find out how you can put your style into action and discover how to 'work the room'.

How to work the room in five easy steps

> *I walk into the room and I look around at everybody and I think, who haven't I spoken to?*
>
> Vanda North, author, speaker,
> global trainer and mind chi inventor

The first rule of working the room is never work the room!

Phew! I'm glad I got that one out of the way. Live networking events are not about collecting business cards, telling as many people as possible all about your business/service/latest offer and it is certainly not about viewing the people there as all that stands between you and a drink at the bar (although there are always exceptions – as you'll see later!)

The phrase 'working the room' emerged at a time when the business world became fixated on the concept of systemizing business. Michael Gerber's excellent *E-Myth* books and business education programmes talked a lot about the need to systemize the activities in your business to enable duplication, economies of scale and efficiency. However, in a networking context, reducing personal interaction with others into a process that is solely focused on a technical outcome will switch those same people off immediately. Think about this from your own perspective just for a moment: how would you feel if someone approached you, shook your hand, thrust a business card into the other and then proceeded to tell you all about themselves for three minutes before looking at their watch and asking you a question to which, as you answer, they are visibly moving away to their next victim? Not great, right? I was going to say that I was exaggerating to make a point here, but I have seen people do this at numerous events. I saw one guy extend this terrible behaviour even further at the end of one event. The room was beginning to empty, I was chatting to a few new business friends and out of the corner of our eyes we could see this guy approaching at pace. 'Sorry to interrupt,' he said, 'I didn't manage to get around everyone. Here is my business card, call me sometime.' Naturally, this individual became a topic of conversation for a minute or two as the group bonded on a new topic of 'Rude Networking 101'. What was he thinking? He had made no connection, he presented himself as someone completely focused on his own outcome and had wasted four business cards.

For the purposes of this chapter, I want you to think of the phrase 'working the room' as a euphemism for networking effectively at live events, whether that be a conference, a dinner, a seminar or a local meeting of your professional association. The purpose of the five steps I am going to outline is to provide you with some structure so that you are not worried about many of the incidentals that make very little difference to your ability to build relationships.

Think about the last great business relationship you formed. How did you meet? Was it planned? What did you talk about when you first met? How did you arrange your second meeting?

My guess is that for many of you, your very best business relationships did not emerge from a formal networking event and if they did, the relationship only moved into the 'great' category over time, accompanied by several drinks maybe and, if you're like my good friend and relationship expert, Gabriele Prestidge, lots of cake! Gabriele is a firm believer in the value of disclosure in her business relationships and it is an interesting concept to bear in mind as you develop any relationship. The people we know and love best and that, vice versa, know and love us best, are intimate to us. While we don't necessarily wish to become really intimate with our network connections, we can still make use of some of the techniques we deploy effortlessly with our closest friends and family – we can share some personal information, we can eat and drink together and, most of all, we can give the relationship time to breathe.

Relationships are not constructed in a workshop, they're cultivated over time.

Introducing the five-step approach

A few years ago, I was invited to run a workshop with a local business group all about networking at live events. We ran through the key components of personal style, the importance of a networking strategy and developing great relationships and all was going great; it felt like there were sufficient 'Aha Moments' and we had a lot of fun identifying some Richard Reds and Yasmin Yellows in the room. I finished up with the five-step approach and then had a chat with a few of the participants. Soon it was time to go but, as I was walking to my car, I felt a tap on my shoulder. I had been followed out of the room by a woman with a huge smile on her face. 'If I hadn't just met you, I would kiss you,' she said (can you guess her networking style?). I tried to tell her that I was happy to forego the formalities, but she was already continuing, 'You have just saved our charity thousands of pounds and, I reckon, we'll be able to exceed all of our targets, no problemo!' I thanked her and was curious to know why she felt this way. 'It's simple,' she said, 'the best networker on our team raises three times more money than anyone else and you have just given me a way of getting everyone up to her standard without needing to invest in lots of training.'

To cut a long story short, that team did exceed all of their targets and even won a national award that year. So, this approach works, give it a try.

The five steps are:

1 Plan

2 Meet

3 Connect

4 Enlist

5 Follow up

Essentially, what we are going to discover is how to make a great first impression and, if you've already made a sound business connection, how to keep developing a great relationship. This is the all-important 'why' of the five-step approach – we want to give ourselves the best possible opportunity of connecting and welcoming valued people into our networks.

Step 1 – Plan

If you are in business, network. There is a word within a word when you're talking networking – that's taking out the 'net' and it is 'working'. So you need to be as prepared when you go networking as you are for any other work that you do and I'm assuming if you're successful that you are very professional at what you do. You're good at what you do and networking is no different.

Mark Perl, trainer in business networking skills,
author of How to Host and Plan Events
and UK LinkedIn trainer

It's not the plan that is important, it's the planning.
Dr Graeme Edwards, Medibank Health Solutions Consultant

That's really what we're talking about here – the process of planning. In planning you will need to think, about the logistics, about your aims from the networking meeting and about the people who may be there. It is the process of thought that will transform your networking, not a written plan. So, let's start at the beginning:

Know who's in the room

It used to be the case that the only events you attended where you knew who would be there, were the ones which either you had organized or events for closed groups of people – ie members only clubs. There is a nice sense of security and excitement in knowing some people before you even turn up. Major face-to-face networks, like Chambers of Commerce, build on this consistency principle, but many more have emerged in recent years; some local, some regional and some national, and all facilitate the process by which great relationships can develop. However, the internet is changing all of that and introducing new opportunities. Many event organizers are now able to share the delegate list with you in advance. Functions like the 'Events' creator on Facebook and business networking sites like Business Scene, make it easy to see who was invited, and, most importantly, who's going. This enables you, using sites like LinkedIn, Twitter and Google+, to find out a bit more about them. Facebook is less helpful here as most people hide their profiles from people with whom they are not connected.

Details such as where they work, who is in their network, what they are proud of, what passions and interests they have and, sometimes, even what they had for breakfast are all discoverable! All of these details are, at the very least, interesting when you are trying to build a profile in your head. In fact, you will probably be able to find out more about them through this quick piece of research, than you would if you met them three or four times.

This initial part of your planning should not just be limited to the people you don't know at the meeting either. Sometimes, something in the lives of the people you have already met will have changed since the last time you saw them too. Maybe they've got a new job, a promotion or started their own business, who knows? However, if you make it your business to keep up to date, you cannot fail but to impress and make them feel special.

Why are you going?

> It's not about the skills of working a room; it's knowing why you're in the
> room in the first place.
>
> Andy Lopata, best-selling author of Recommended:
> How to sell through networking and referrals *and*
> *leading business networking strategist*

Asking yourself 'WHY?' is the first step towards developing a networking strategy, but let's not get ahead of ourselves. At this stage, understanding 'why' you have decided to attend a particular event is a very valid question and if the answer is 'I don't know', then now is the time to pause and think of a good reason. Having written a book all about personal effectiveness, I guess you would expect me to ask you to use your time well. Whether you are networking on behalf of your employer, for your own business or just simply to gain some exposure for yourself, thinking through how a particular live networking event can help you towards your goal(s) is a good idea. Here are three good reasons that immediately spring to mind, I'm sure you'll have others:

1   To socialize – I've put this one first because there are many more
opportunities to attend social events than there are business
meetings and it's not a bad idea to start thinking of them as
great networking opportunities too. I met one of the loveliest
people in my life (Christina Bush) at a purely social dinner
and that has led to working together on a number of projects.

However, having a social aim for a business networking event is sometimes a good idea too, as it is effectively a subset of potential reason 2...

2   To build existing relationships – I always find it curious when people have advised me not to talk to the people that I know at events. This only makes sense if you are viewing your fellow networkers as targets for business card distribution. Obviously, there will be people beyond your friends and other contacts at the event that you will want to meet, but don't be in such a hurry that you put at risk the growing connection you have with your existing network. Relax, listen carefully and enjoy the conversations – the reason you made contact in the first place is because you wanted to explore the opportunities to support each other, so deepening the sense of connection and finding out more about them and their current goals will only enhance the relationship even more. As a secondary benefit, you may find that you even attract new people to you. There is nothing more attractive than someone smiling and having fun.

3   To learn something from someone – I could have just said to learn something, but of course you can do that at home on your own. As someone who has spent most of my career helping people to acquire knowledge and, in the process, learning even more myself, I can definitely say that learning from others is far easier, and much more enjoyable, than conducting research on Wikipedia! Some networks are set up especially to facilitate social learning and, while you may think that this could limit the opportunities to build relationships, the opposite is actually true. Discussing issues, concepts and strategies is a great way of creating a solid and informed connection with others.

4   To meet new contacts – well, if you really have to! I don't think I need to cover the 'why' of this one, but if you want some ideas on 'how' to do this effectively, stay with me.

You'll notice that I didn't list 'To do some business'. You may have a business goal of making more sales, but if you have that as your intention from a networking event, you may be disappointed. Chet Holmes, author of the brilliant *Ultimate Sales Machine* has estimated that only 3 per cent of any group are looking to buy at any one time and even they will resist being 'sold to'. Don't waste your time, go make some great friends and guess who they will think of first when they are looking to buy?

Logistics

This is a really important topic, especially if you are new to networking and a little bit nervous, because it can make you feel a lot more confident, immediately. Start with what you are going to wear – what is the dress code? In general, business casual is a fine default for most business networking events, but there may be differences, so always check if you are not keen on standing out in the crowd. Other things to consider are: knowing whether you need to register beforehand; the location of the event; the start time; and how close you will be able to park or how far you will need to walk from public transport. Your aim is to arrive early, looking bright and breezy and ready to have a great time. I always arrive early whenever I join a new group because it gives me an excuse to talk to the organizer and ask if there is anything I can do to help. Straight away you will make a new friend and, even if there is nothing for you to do, you can be sure that they will know someone perfect for you to meet.

Preparation

It may seem odd to cover this at the end of the section on planning, but in many ways, it is the least important. What we are going to look at here are a few things that you may wish to take with you, but none of them are critical. In fact, if you forget any of them, what a great excuse to follow up any connections you make with a second face-to-face meeting.

1   Business cards – having said that you don't want to be thrusting business cards into the hands of the people you meet at live events (the number 1 pet hate of most of our experts); it makes complete sense to have some with you in case any of your conversations develop to the point at which one or both of you wish to follow up with the other. I have to say that, from a personal perspective, I have rarely requested a business card because I have always been a fan of capturing information digitally. Sometimes, it is quicker to take a card, but I always enter the details onto my phone as soon as possible and then file the card away. What sort of business card you have may not be up to you if you work for someone else, but if you work for yourself, the card itself is less important than the way in which you present it to someone. If you are exchanging cards, stop the conversation, read their card and make a comment of some sort. Write on it if there is something you have agreed to do in terms of follow-up, but, whatever you do, try to add some element of emotion to the process so that you will recall both the individual and the conversation better. Your actions

will typically initiate the same action from them and help them remember you better when they get home.

2   Information – many business events will provide an opportunity for you to bring information and either display it or add it to the infamous 'goody bag'. This is where we could venture into the world of marketing so I will resist commenting on the effectiveness of this strategy. All I am saying by adding it to this list, is that if this is something you are planning to do, contact the organizer in advance to check out the best approach.

3   Enlisting words – this is something that we will cover in more detail in Step 4 – Enlist, but it is included in this list to reassure you that, while it is good to have a few simple and clear things to say about what you do, it really doesn't make a lot of difference if you don't say it perfectly when you meet people. People like people, not rehearsed speeches. In fact, being too rehearsed can have the opposite effect and give the impression that you are too slick! Strive to just be yourself and get excited about what you do. This will communicate what you are all about far more effectively than any pre-rehearsed words. Thinking about what you want to communicate generally is a good idea though, especially if there is someone at the event you particularly want to meet.

Step 2 – Meet

What people say and feel about you when you've left a room is precisely your job while you are in it.

Rasheed Ogunlaru, business coach, speaker, writer, author of Soul Trader

If our goal is to build great relationships with the people in our networks, then the very first step towards doing this is making a memorable first impression. Quite often, your fellow networkers will meet many people when they attend a live meeting, so making a good connection is vital. However, there are many ways to do this, so I thought I would share the main ones mentioned by our experts to get you started.

Be different

This, in many ways, is the most obvious way of being remembered after the networking event. How can you dress to stand out? We're not talking about being dressed inappropriately here or wearing something ridiculous; it's more about what accessories you can wear that will initiate a conversation and stick in the minds of the people you meet. The focus here is on the visual. The incredible Vanda North, at the time of writing, has a splash of shocking pink through her hair – this is not only memorable, but accentuates her message of self-confidence as she spreads her joy around the world.

I have often told the story of a network contact of mine who took to carrying an umbrella with him everywhere. Those of you familiar with the climate in the UK may think this is a normal thing to do, but the interesting thing was, he took it to events when the sun was actually making its annual appearance! For people he'd never met before, he was 'the guy with the umbrella' and not another face in the crowd.

I've seen hats, fob watches, bracelets, brooches, odd writing instruments, brightly coloured files, unique handbags, waistcoats, bright trousers and jackets, pink shirts (Thomas Power), flamboyant ties, T-shirts (Brad Burton) and close up magic with business cards. It all works, but do your best to be natural in the process. The reality is, these days in business there are ever diminishing expectations as to how you 'should' present yourself. Thanks to the prominence of exceedingly successful informal individuals such as Steve Jobs, Mark Zuckerberg and Richard Branson, the world has become a less stuffy place, so you decide how you want to dress.

To reinforce the benefit of wearing something memorable, let me share an anecdote from one of our experts, Susan Mumford:

SUSAN MUMFORD!

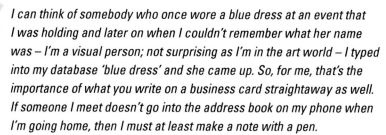

> I can think of somebody who once wore a blue dress at an event that I was holding and later on when I couldn't remember what her name was – I'm a visual person; not surprising as I'm in the art world – I typed into my database 'blue dress' and she came up. So, for me, that's the importance of what you write on a business card straightaway as well. If someone I meet doesn't go into the address book on my phone when I'm going home, then I must at least make a note with a pen.
>
> Susan Mumford, founder of Be Smart About Art
> and the Association of Women Art Dealers

The second way you can be different is in the way you introduce yourself. The temptation is to lead with your job title but very few people will know what you do, or they will assume you do exactly the same job as someone else they know with the same job title. Instead, think about the results you achieve or the difference you make to your clients.

> Introduce yourself in Technicolor. It is the point of the first few words you say, you've just got to get people interested to ask you another question and start a conversation effectively.
>
> I will give you an example. I met this lady for the first time. She was probably in the late 50s, maybe early 60s, that sort of age, a very slight lady. I said to her, 'Hi there.' I introduced myself and she said, 'Hi there. I'm Jill. I'm a weightlifter.' I looked at her and I said, 'What?' I could only ask. 'Tell me more.' When we talked about it, she said, 'I'm a

*weightlifter. I lift the weights off people's shoulders. I'm a stress
counsellor.' That's introducing yourself in Technicolor. If she said, 'Hi
there. I'm a stress counsellor,' I might have wanted to know more
but there is a real risk that I wouldn't ask a question. I wouldn't really
engage in a conversation.*

Charlie Lawson, National Director of BNI in the UK and Ireland

Be yourself

It is very tempting when attending a business networking event to don a
new persona along with your business clothes, but this is a serious mistake.
The main reason people do this is because they worry that they are not
impressive enough, or not engaging enough but nothing could be further
from the truth. Yes, you need a little bit of confidence but this is not to
overcome a weakness, this is to give yourself the best opportunity to display
your strengths. When you relax, the people you meet will relax and warm
to you. I think the following example hits the nail on the proverbial head.

*When I go to business events I just treat them as a party. The difference
between going to a social event and a business event is very simple.
The amount of alcohol you consume or don't consume. Other than that
I always treat them as a party. Just have fun, just relax but most of all
be yourself. Don't try to act. Be who you are. There is a great quote
from a senior business development director from a massive law firm;
he said to me once: 'Do you know the problem with lawyers when they*

go networking?'. I said, 'No, go on tell me.'. He said, 'The problem with lawyers when they go networking is that they behave like lawyers and not like the nice people they are.'. That sort of encapsulates what people try to do.

Will Kintish, author of I Hate Networking

Be helpful

I mentioned earlier the obvious value in helping the organizer of an event if you can, but don't do this if your heart is not in it. Be true to yourself and if that means being genuinely concerned for others or wishing to help, then this too can become a point of differentiation. One of the first people I met when I moved to the south coast of England a few years back was an incredibly caring person called Helen Jeffery. Helen was always introducing people and offering her services if she saw something needed to be done. Her reputation spread faster than almost anyone else I knew at that time and the charity she worked for never struggled to attract PR and a steady flow of supporters. If you're just getting started, offer any help you can; connect your new contacts, direct people to the rest rooms, the coffees, the organizers or the tables. It's an easy way to meet new friends and a guaranteed way to at least start a conversation or initiate a new relationship. I call this the caring principle; people don't care how much you know until they know how much you care, so find ways to demonstrate that you genuinely care!

Accentuate features

Do you think you would have forgotten if you'd met Robert Pershing Wadlow at a networking event? Robert was 8'11.1" and 35 stone and is still the tallest man that ever lived (or at least since records began). Some people have easily recognizable and distinguishable features and if you are lucky enough to fall into this category then don't hide your light under a bushel, accentuate it. It's a free ticket to many memorable meetings – even your less flattering features.

Step 3 – Connect

The irrepressible Andy Lopata has a newsletter called 'Connecting is not enough' and I couldn't agree more, but how do you go about making the connection in the first place? Well, if your dazzling smile, sharp dressing and smooth charm hasn't even troubled their radar, there is still hope. As with much of what we have discussed already in this book, it is all about your mindset. Once you are clear that you are not at a networking event to sell, either yourself or your wares, then it is easy to focus on 'giving' first.

The gift of the present

When you meet someone for the first time, the initial gifts you are going to give them are your attention and your time. Be present, listen to what they have to say, make the odd note if you wish, but utilize, what Eckhart Tolle calls, 'the power of now' and zero in on the person to whom you are talking. Try to switch off that part of your brain that wants you to interrupt and tell them all about you and instead focus on how you may be able to help them – the second gift you can offer. Who among your existing connections would be of value to them? What industry or functional information are you aware of that may make an impact on them or their business? Have you, or any close contacts, faced and solved any similar issues to the ones being tackled by your new connection? This is active listening at its best; you are demonstrating that you are paying attention by thinking of appropriate opportunities for them. This won't always work, sometimes you won't have anything to offer other than your friendship and sometimes, this is all that they need. Still, continue to listen and make mental notes because there may be something that comes in via a different network channel later, that will be perfect for them.

 Whenever somebody says to me, 'I feel really uncomfortable about networking. I just don't know what to say,' I always believe, great,

*we found someone for whom networking is going to work, once they
appreciate the skill they bring by being a listener.*

*Dinah Liversidge, co-founder of #thebreakfastclub
and Executive Business Mentor*

A note on disclosure

Once the conversation does come around to you, try not to be a 'closed
book'. People like people who are warm and easy to communicate with and
the best way to help them like you is to share some information that is not
necessarily all about business. How did you get to the event this evening?
Did you experience any challenges? What's keeping you awake at night?
What's exciting you about your business or personal life right now? What
are you hoping for in the near future? What are you having for dinner later?
Even the most mundane aspects of life, like this last topic, can increase the
sense of connection between two people; after all, it's what makes us human.
Just be careful to not sound like you are complaining about everything. Get
the balance right between any negative aspects of your conversation and
the positive items. Again, you want people to enjoy the time they spend
with you so that they will be inspired to spend more time with you in the
future. In this vein, it is also worth remembering that, while disclosing some
personal information is good from the point of view of connecting, over-
sharing can have a detrimental effect, so be careful.

Before you go

If you've made a great connection, make sure you remember to finish the
conversation in style by exchanging contact details and noting any points
of follow up. These days, the list of contact details can be extensive, but it's
definitely worth the trouble to capture their social media details along with
their phone and e-mail address. Alternatively, you can ask them to send you
these bits of information in the follow-up e-mail. Of course, as a budding
networking professional, all of your details will be in your e-mail signature!

Step 4 – Enlist

There will come a point in the conversation with your new connection when
they will ask, 'What do you do?' and so a little forethought might be useful.
You don't want to spend 10 minutes explaining in endless detail every aspect

of your job or role, but, likewise, this is not necessarily an elevator pitch that needs to blurted out in less than 10 seconds and is, therefore, over before the other person has even tuned in to your answer. Ideally, you're aiming for something between 15 and 90 seconds. You'll be at the shorter end of that scale if you have something really dynamic or unusual to share that will prompt a second question, and the longer end of the scale if you have a really great anecdote to add texture to your answer.

Whatever you answer, the reason I've called this step 'enlist' is because this is your first opportunity to provide the other person with the information they would need to generate referrals for you. However, I would like to emphasize the word 'first' here. There will be many opportunities for your connection to get to know all about what you do as your relationship grows and the odds are only moderate on them being able to make an immediate referral for you and your business. Generally, people like to refer their friends, but even friends need to have a good story to tell if they are going to refer you successfully. So let's look at what our experts suggest.

Message in a bottle

Your message needs to have two distinct features:

1 It needs to give the listener the sense that there is a specific buyer for your goods or services, maybe it's them or someone they can think of?

2 It needs to be memorable.

The key is to provide a statement illustrating how you can help people or businesses overcome a specific challenge. Here's a format for your message that seems to have stood the test of time:

 I specialize in... I work with... helping them to... For example,...

Once you have worked out how you can fill the gaps with your information, you can vary the format and personalize it even more. As long as you are helping them get a visual cue on a potential client, then you've done your job well. Here are a couple of examples to give you a sense of what you are aiming to achieve:

 I specialize in increasing profit for small retail businesses. I work with busy shop owners and help them reduce costs and expand their local market. For example, I've been helping a local picture framing business owner to double profits over the last year through product

diversification and opening up new digital media channels. Just one Twitter campaign brought in 15 per cent more customers.

I specialize in boosting the happiness of people stuck in care homes through cost effective activities that care home owners love too. I provide in-house art and craft sessions for the residents to help them to gain a sense of accomplishment and camaraderie adding to the variety of activities provided by the care home owners. For example, one care home I work with has residents with severe mental health issues that mean they do not normally interact with others. We ran some card making sessions which engaged many of the residents for the first time in months.

This last example is a real one that the wonderful Kathy Toop emerged with when we worked on this for her social enterprise. It immediately makes you think, who do I know that owns a care home, works with care home owners or has a relative in a care home? Any one of the questions could lead to a great referral for Kathy.

Sometimes a quick check question at the end of your message will enable you to assess if the individual has really understood what you are saying. Something like, 'Does that make sense?' or 'Do you know anyone that might need a service like that?'

Once you've shared your message, offer your card because now it has a purpose. Even better, ask for their card with the sole intent of following up with them or seeking out referrals that might add value to them.

At the start of this section, I suggested that the enlisting process starts when you are asked what you do – don't jump the gun and tell them this information if you are not asked though. You'll be able to slip into the conversation some examples of what you do without needing a formal prompt, so focus instead on nudging the relationship forward. What else can you give your new connection? When are you going to meet again? Will you see them at the next event or sooner? Having a long-term perspective and investing in others in this way will ensure you build a solid and substantial network.

Step 5 – Follow up

Before we take a look at the various aspects of following up with your new connections, let me just emphasize how important this step is in our sequence. Every single one of our networking experts identified following up as a critical ingredient to their success in developing great relationships. However, in my experience, it is an aspect of networking which is hugely overlooked and this is your opportunity to differentiate yourself from the masses of people who don't do it well.

According to the latest statistics we are bombarded with over 20,000 pieces of information a day! This includes things we hear on the radio and in conversations and things we see on the television or on the internet, not to mention the plethora of advertising we are subjected to almost incessantly. So, is it any wonder that sometimes we forget both a conversation and the person we were speaking to, just hours after the event? Following up is the bridge between your meetings and the next meeting but, if you are smart, it can be an opportunity to provide incredible value, all on its own! We learn and retain information best through repetition, so if you want to stay in the minds of the people in your network once you've made a connection, think of 'follow up' as a continuous process rather than a one-off event. So where do we start?

Same day

Social media has transformed the way we are able to build strong foundations for our new relationships. We can take pictures at an event and share them with the world in seconds. All of the most popular tools allow status updates and what better way of sharing your network than announcing who you have just met? With the longer updates available on everything except Twitter, you could also invite responses if there is a particular issue the individual has that you think someone else in your network may be able to help with.

So, the bottom line is, connect with them immediately on the main online networks that they use and initiate an online conversation as soon as possible. In one quick and easy routine, you have just fulfilled the two purposes of follow up: to create a bridge between the first and second live connections and to remind them of who you are. 'Genius!' as my mate and fellow author (he likes that title), Nick Smith would say.

Next day

If you made a careful note of who you could introduce from your network to your new contact, now is the time to do it. The details of who, why and what will be fresh in your mind and you will be communicating to all concerned that this is a high priority for you. Make your introduction generous, after all, it costs nothing and it will really brighten the day of both of the parties involved. Personally, I love introducing people because it gives me a wonderful opportunity to sing their praises in a completely transparent way without causing anyone too much embarrassment. Your contacts are pretty special too – look who they've all got in common in their networks!

The second thing you can do to follow up is send through any promised documents, links or resources. Even if you didn't promise anything, it doesn't hurt to send through something that you think may be helpful. My favourite is links to books that I hope will add some value. Do the job properly, and one sentence of explanation is all you need to save them several minutes of trying to remember why you are sending this particular nugget through.

Soon

If someone committed to sending something through to you, don't panic if it doesn't arrive immediately. Remember, you are in an elite group of super networkers and not everyone aspires to be so effective. There's no harm following up with a quick reminder a few days after the event if you haven't heard back. It's very likely that life just got in the way.

The best next step you can make after meeting someone at an event, is to meet them again for a one to one. This time, you can relax a bit more and get to know them just a little better. All of the great ideas you implemented under Step 3 – Connect (see page 57) are still relevant; being present, listening with intent, sharing your networks and a good mix of social and business. The additional opportunities as you get to know people better are the insights into their values, beliefs and aspirations as well as greater awareness of the specific challenges they may be facing right now, that they were perhaps reluctant to share in a first meeting.

Be open, share your hopes and fears and maybe even discuss your ideal referrals. This last topic in particular is always a good one because, very often, people haven't given it a lot of thought.

Before I finish this topic I wanted to share an acronym that a good friend of mine uses all the time to help people in his industry to get the most out of their live networking.

Mark Lee is a network facilitator for tax experts and accountants and is a real expert in his field. He also happens to be one of the nicest people you'll ever be fortunate enough to bump into! I asked all of our experts what they avoid when networking and many talked of individuals thrusting business cards into their hands, but what else should you avoid?

Five things you should AVOID doing when you're at a business networking event:

A = Asking for work – unless you already know the person you are speaking to as you first need to build some trust.

V = Visually scanning the room – you need to appear interested in the person you're speaking with or they won't be interested in you either.

O = Outstaying your welcome – especially true if the person you're with knows more people than you do.

I = Ignoring answers – be more interested in listening than in talking if you're serious about building a relationship and generating referrals.

D = Defeating the purpose – by failing to follow up. It will make all the difference.

So there it is, five steps to working a room, where working the room is nothing more than building your network effectively, one great relationship at a time. Do that a few times a month, including the social events you attend, and pretty soon you will have an enviable network.

Key points

The mark of a good conversationalist is not that you can talk a lot. The mark is that you can get others to talk a lot. Thus, good schmoozers are good listeners, not good talkers.

Guy Kawasaki, author, speaker, investor,
business adviser and former chief evangelist of Apple

The five-step approach is your key to networking effectively at live events with the most important step being 'follow up'.

Following up has never been easier and in the next chapter we will explore the best tools for the job.

Tools for the job

We shape our tools and our tools shape us.
Wilson Miner, former digital product designer at Facebook

Eleven years ago I wrote a chapter in *Time Management 24/7* all about how the world was going to change and how easy it would be in the future to work with people across different time zones, from different continents and cultures. At that time, most people only had e-mail but there were a few pioneers that were forging ahead with websites that enabled people to come together to reconnect with old friends, meet new people and build meaningful relationships online. In the short period since then, the industry of relationship facilitation has swept all before it. Networking, social media, industry forums and dating sites account for the vast majority of web traffic across the globe and now, through the integration of 'comment boxes' on many business websites, the rest of the web is catching up too. Coupled with the ubiquitous use of mobile phones for talking and texting, the opportunity to interact with people at any time of the day, in any part of the world, is staggering.

How can you squander even one more day not taking advantage of the greatest shifts of our generation? How dare you settle for less when the world has made it so easy for you to be remarkable?
Seth Godin, author of Small Is the New Big: And 183 other riffs, rants, and remarkable business ideas

Seth was talking in terms of marketing, but the quote equally applies to any personal aspirations you have too. Regardless of what you need to find out, who you would like to meet, what you would like to discuss, there is a place on the internet for you to find it. In this chapter, I'm going to give you a high level view of some of the most prominent tools at your disposal today in the full knowledge that some of the details will be out of date by the time you read this! However, what I have done is to garner the insights of some of the world's leading exponents of these tools so that you can decide which ones you would like to explore further right now. If I can spark your interest, I know from experience, that you will be willing to put in the time to explore any new features, or indeed new tools, that appear long after today.

Facebook

 At Facebook, we build tools to help people connect with the people they want and share what they want, and by doing this we are extending people's capacity to build and maintain relationships.
Mark Zuckerberg, founder and CEO of Facebook

With over a billion users, Facebook is by far the biggest online network in the world. The ability to share information, photos and news with friends, old and new, now seems to be almost passé. Not that the usage is slowing down; in fact, the latest reports suggest that, on average, people use Facebook for more than eight hours a month – that's the average, so some are online much more than that. When it was growing, observers were fascinated by where the audience was coming from, as tribes and networks moved en masse from other platforms such as MySpace, Friendster and Friends Reunited. Now the conversation is more about who will win the battle for our mobile phones. As I look out the window from my wi-fi enabled coffee shop, at least every other person has evolved to the point where they can walk through a crowded train station, texting or writing status updates for their networks, without bumping into anyone. It seems our peripheral vision is developing at the same rate as our thumb dexterity!

In many ways, Facebook has popularized the concept of networking. Formerly the restricted domain of business people, almost everyone is at it now! The great thing is that most people, when left to their own devices (pardon the pun), network more effectively than they do when they decide to network. The reason, as you will have anticipated, is because they're just focusing on the relationship rather than any specific outcome. People share the intimate details of their lives and join in the timelines of their friends purely because they want to connect. They are responding to their very natural desire to engage with their fellow human beings.

So, when it comes to networking, we're all starting from a level playing field on Facebook. Within minutes we can set up an account and share a photo or comment on someone else's 'Wall', or even wish someone Happy Birthday! We can connect to family, close friends and discover old friends effortlessly as Facebook suggests people you may know based on who you connect to initially, and your friends suggest others that you may want to connect with. Thereafter, how you utilize the functionality of Facebook to build your relationships and your networks is up to you. For many, expanding beyond this point is fraught with fear – particularly when it comes to matters of privacy. To help you along, here are some top tips on how to get the most out of Facebook, while maintaining a degree of control, if that is your choice.

Sort your friends out!

It is very easy to add people as friends on Facebook; so easy in fact that many people hesitate for fear of what that will mean for their ability to share information. How do you respond when your work colleague sends you a friend request, especially if that colleague is your boss? Well, if you want options, we need to go back a few steps and do some preparation.

There are just two steps to setting up your Facebook account so that you can use it confidently. The first is to create a few categories of Friends and the second is to remember to put people in those categories. Friend categories can be set up in privacy settings and for each category you can decide what they see of your content. Once a category has been set up, you can click on an individual friend and simply add them to it. For new friends, you may need to accept their friend request before you can assign them to one or more of your categories (depending on whether you are on a computer or a web-enabled phone).

Thereafter, when you add content via a status update or a photograph, you can select which category of friends see it. So, for example, if you wish to share photos just with close family and friends, you would create that category and select it each time you add a new photo. This degree of audience segmentation is also offered on Google+ but not LinkedIn currently.

Like what you see

The aim of using Facebook from the perspective of building relationships is to share information with your friends and to keep yourself up to date with what your friends are doing in their lives. Photos are probably the most important aspect of this process and typically, an update with a photo is commented on more than a straightforward text update at a ratio of about 4:1. The quickest way to indicate to your friends that you have seen their photos is to click the 'Like' button underneath the photo. They can see you have liked their photo and obviously read any comment you have written too.

Play tag

Once you have mastered the simple task of adding a photo or writing an update, you can start engaging your friends more directly by 'tagging' them. Basically, as you write your update or add a photo, you merely start typing their name and Facebook offers you the opportunity to select them from a suggested list of your friends. This inserts their name into your update and means that they will have an option to see your update in their own timeline. Depending on your mutual privacy settings, your update may then be visible to their friends (if they want it to be and you have allowed it to be). Some people overthink this activity and worry if their updates are interesting or how their friends will respond, but the key is to just be yourself and post anything that interests you or you think might interest a particular friend. This is a great way of interacting with people who might be too busy to talk right now or in a different time zone.

A good, old-fashioned, letter

As well as being able to use the Instant Message system, Facebook also provides a private message service that enables you to simply write to your friends if you have something longer than a short update to communicate. If there are time differences to overcome, this process works brilliantly and, for many people, has eliminated the need for e-mails.

Google+

Up until recently, this was the commonly understood perception of Google+:

Google+ is the gym of social networking: We all join, but nobody actually uses it.

Unknown

I'm sure Mark Zuckerberg would have liked it to have stayed that way. However, Google+ is on the march and a lot of industry insiders are now predicting that Google+ could win the battle for our attention by a country mile. Every week, I read revised headlines on when Google+ will hit the magical 1 billion users.

One of the best thing about Google+ so far, is the ease with which you can add your connections to their way of segmenting your connections, called circles. Close friends, acquaintances, colleagues, neighbours, clubs, business associates can all be segmented enabling you to choose who gets to see your updates. When you add a connection on Google+ you have to put them into a circle which, many of the users I interviewed said, feels more secure to them than the Facebook approach. This simple segmentation means that you can easily utilize Google+ for business and social purposes.

Anyone with a Gmail account can have a Google+ account and the added integration with YouTube and indeed most web content means that you can share almost anything you find while surfing the net. This is not Google's first attempt at developing an online networking tool, but it is by far the most complete.

From a personal promotion perspective, Google+ is holding a trump card. If you want people to find you as part of your personal networking strategy, then being active on Google+ is a smart thing to do. Everything you post on Google+ is indexed and therefore discoverable across the web. The same used to be true of Ecademy, which actually preceded all of the modern social business networks. Blogs, articles and even comments that are posted in the public spaces are visible to anyone conducting a search. Like LinkedIn, which we will look at next, Google+ is a great place to be if you run a small- to medium-sized business, but the benefits to individuals are worth investigating too. The important thing is not to confuse broadcasting with networking. It's still all about building relationships – who can you help? Who can you introduce? Who can you inspire? Where can you add value?

LinkedIn

 Active participation on LinkedIn is the best way to say, 'Look at me!' without saying 'Look at me!'

Bobby Darnell, founder and principal of Construction Market Consultants, Inc

CASE STUDY

Earlier we discussed the merits of a more open approach to networking and I thought it would be useful to share how it can work for you based on an example I heard today. A new associate of mine told me that six months ago he clicked on one of those 'suggested connections' on LinkedIn. The other person accepted and they started a brief online conversation in which she asked him if he was available for a new opportunity that had arisen at her company. At the time he was employed and had to decline, but more recently he was made redundant and reached out to his network to see what was going on. Initially, he did not hear back from this random connection but at the start of this week, she made contact and he's just been offered a contract worth many times more than anything he has ever earned before. You just never know!

LinkedIn is known as *the* online business network. Thousands of new users sign up each day to include themselves in the largest business database in use today. Initially, people signed up and merely added a bunch of business details about themselves in a format very similar to a curriculum vitae; today this is the bare minimum you will want to do if you wish to maximize the networking potential of this tool.

Every LinkedIn expert I interviewed, recommended that you start with the basics:

- Put a photo up as soon as you register. It helps to build trust, attract viewers to your profile, add credibility and character. A straightforward head and shoulders shot is fine.

- Write your headline – make it as descriptive as you can as this too can be used by other users to find you.

From here you need to complete the rest of your profile, remembering to add schools, further education and your vocational activities alongside each of your (dated) jobs.

Once your basics are sorted out, you can begin to explore the host of other features on LinkedIn that can help you build your professional networks. Here are some of the favourite functions and top tips from our experts:

Groups

This is where you can really start to add and exchange value with your network online. Groups are formed for a variety of reasons and usually around industry specialisms or shared interests. However, there are also many that are just a 'shop window' for particular businesses. This is okay if you have an interest in that business, but not much use to you if you are thinking of using the groups to grow your network.

The simplest reason to join groups is that they expose you to a bigger group of people than you may be connected to personally. You can interact with any members of the group and, if you wish, send them a connection request based on your mutual membership of the group.

I would suggest that people review their use of groups. People seem to join groups because they think that somehow that's going to expose them to a broader audience. Well unfortunately, the joining doesn't; it's the activity that does. Only join a group if you're actually

*going to be active and you're going to be able to add something of
value to the group.*

Linda Parkinson-Hardman, author of LinkedIn Made Easy *and
founder and CEO of The Hysterectomy Association*

When Linda talks of being active in your groups, she is talking about
responding to requests from within the group or contributing ideas, links
and data that will benefit the other members of the group. I'm sure Linda
would also advocate the following advice from another LinkedIn author
and expert, Bert Verdonck:

*One of the most powerful things you can do on LinkedIn is to post
someone's question in your status update with a link to the group
where it was asked. The relevant expert in your network then gets
an opportunity to display their knowledge and receives a warm
introduction to the group, who now see them as an expert on that
particular topic. Everyone's reputation is enhanced with this strategy.*

Bert Verdonck, co-author of How to REALLY Use LinkedIn

Choosing which groups to join and then getting the most from them is
viewed by many as the biggest challenge on LinkedIn, but James Potter, the
self-styled 'LinkedIn Man', insists that this shouldn't be difficult:

*I have actually 64 groups on LinkedIn that people think I spend my life
in. The truth is I don't. I get through the interactions in 64 groups in
about 25, 30 minutes. It's about having an approach to that and how you
interact with that.*

One of the things I find fascinating with people's interaction in groups is they notably join groups full of people that look like them. So you take accountants, there's currently 1,220 groups for accountants on LinkedIn and they're all full of accountants. I wonder why there are no clients there? If you want to meet with clients, go where clients go. Don't go where you go, which is where we all naturally tend to gravitate.

The other thing that I find fascinating about groups is the number of times I see people going into a group and shouting, 'Buy my stuff. I am great.' That also won't work.

James Potter, 'The LinkedIn Man' – strategic business adviser

Whenever you pop into a group on LinkedIn, just be yourself. The mindset we discussed in Chapter 4 is completely relevant here. Think of it as just a room full of people. Listen to the conversations, join in a few debates and, where possible, help your fellow members. By showing up regularly, people will begin to trust you and you will build the same great relationships that you do offline. Just remember, that it takes time. This is not a once in a while activity. Little and often is a canny strategy when building relationships. So, as James says, plan your approach to groups so that you can literally just pop your head around the proverbial door and rekindle your relationships. Once you get into the swing of things, you will pick up the tone of the group and begin to know intuitively how you can help the members, what they like and how they like it.

Profile

Don't just stick to boring professional information when writing your profile. We used to have a guideline of 50:50 on Ecademy (50 per cent professional and 50 per cent personal information). I don't think you necessarily need that balance on LinkedIn, but something that expresses your personality and provides additional points of connection is obviously a bonus.

 Most people just put their function or the title and the company they work for but it's also important to add some flavour to it. For example one of the things I have in my professional headline is 'Happy Chocoholic'. So of course I can state, 'Hey my name is Bert and I'm a chocoholic.' You would be surprised how many people just contact me talking about chocolate first, before we talk about business.
Bert Verdonck, co-author of How to REALLY Use LinkedIn

Your profile is the equivalent of your introduction to the many people you will meet inside LinkedIn, so be generous with the information you share. If you have a particular expertise, load up some tips or ideas using the slide share functionality or direct people to your blog if you prefer to write. You really cannot overdo it; people will choose for themselves how much they explore your content.

Twitter

 The qualities that make Twitter seem inane and half-baked are what makes it so powerful.
Jonathan Zittrain, Professor of Law at Harvard Law School, social theorist and author of The Future of the Internet

The non-Twitter user's perspective of this strange phenomenon is that it is filled with people sharing what they had for breakfast or what they think of the latest reality TV star – and, for a large proportion of the users, this would be an accurate assumption. However, like all good truths, the opposite can also be stated with a degree of certainty. Twitter is also home to some of the most creative marketing campaigns in the world and is an amazingly powerful networking tool. Twitter is the only place on the web currently that you can send a message to any other user that will almost certainly hit the target.

For anyone who's never used Twitter, it is a short messaging service that allows you to update the world with a message of no more than 140 characters. Initially, this seems impossibly short and when you progress to the next level of including others' names and hash-tags, it's even worse! However, within a very short space of time, you can master it. Here are a few of the rules, written in Twitter format, to show you how easy it is:

- Maximum message length = 140 characters. Characters include punctuation.

- A hashtag is simply something that adds your tweet to a particular conversation, eg #London2012 was popular during the last Olympic Games.

- Hashtags are also used to add emphasis to a specific point, like #tweetinglikeapro

- You choose a Twitter username and the format is @1simonphillips. This appears in all of your messages.

- Your profile picture is shown alongside every tweet, so make it a good one!

- Your full information is shown if people look at your profile, not just your tweet. URL web links are sent in full, unless you use a shortening service like bit.ly

- If you want to say 'Hi!' to a friend or send them a link, you just add their Twitter name to the message, eg Hi @keithkeller

- People search for content on Twitter by typing #hashtags and @names.

- You can follow anyone on Twitter and then see what they are tweeting about through your home screen timeline.

- You can send private 'direct' messages to people on Twitter, but only if they've followed you.

- Including someone's @name in your message will make it visible to them through their connect tab and also to anyone else searching for their content.

- If you see something good, you can RT (retweet) it to your followers.

- Pictures can be attached to tweets. #addingmoreinterest.

My personal introduction to the power of Twitter was during the UK general election of 2010. I had been registered on Twitter for some time but confined my involvement to a few tweets and retweets of words that I thought others might find useful. However, I tuned in on election night and started reading the tweets that were flooding in under hash tags like #ukelection. It was phenomenal. I suddenly realized that the network on Twitter was significantly ahead of the 'live' news programmes on the TV, as people in the polling stations started sharing results. Not only that, but the comments were much more engaging and passionate. It felt like a conversation you might have had in the pub or over dinner.

Indeed, the speed of Twitter is its main feature. You can engage with almost anyone in seconds without needing to join groups, circles or pages. For example, a little while ago, I would regularly join in a conversation called #thebreakfastclub hosted by some amazingly inspirational friends of mine, @DinahLiversidge and @JayneMCox. It is largely focused on setting people up to have a fantastic day, but they also wanted to support and promote a few charities as the conversation grew and more people popped into their virtual café. I knew a charity that would love to be promoted, so I made the introduction and the whole thing was set up in minutes. Whatever your interests, there is almost certainly a conversation going on that you can observe and contribute to at almost any time. Back to Dinah:

I search for topics that I love reading about, chatting about, challenging, hearing about, and so I see who's talking about them. I find out who's talking about them, see who I know that's connected to those people

and I connect. It's very rare that I choose to connect with somebody online because of what they do for business.

Dinah Liversidge, coach, mentor and connector

Using this and other strategies, I have made lots of great connections on Twitter and even publish a daily magazine. The magazine is a great example of a networking win–win; it draws content from inspirational and knowledge-building articles, blogs and pictures referenced in the tweets of an amazing network of people around the world who share my philosophy of everyone can make a difference (http://paper.li/1simonphillips/making-a-difference). I am able to promote the contributors to my network and provide tons of inspirational and informative content in the process.

CASE STUDY

So, let's have a look at the top five Twitter tips of Twitter expert Keith Keller:

1 Be a resource not a salesperson.

2 Set up your profile well. Your bio is like your elevator pitch, it communicates what you do to others in less than 15 seconds.

3 Make sure that there's a link. Make sure that you've got all your links, so that if someone comes to your page and says, 'Hey, actually, I'm interested in that. I've been meaning to find out more about that,' and then there's no link. Remember people are busy. They haven't got time to e-mail you or find your e-mail address or go to your website or Google you. They haven't got time. You've got to make it easy for people.

4 Get outside your circle. Don't confine yourself to the people you already know. It's a global opportunity.

5 Find your niche. I used to be a career counsellor and people would say to me, 'I will do anything.' Well, OK. But if I meet someone, it's unlikely they're going to say, 'Do you know anyone that can do anything?' For me, it's Twitter, not Google+, Pinterest or YouTube. If the subject of Twitter comes up, then I will be in your mind, burned into your brain. Keith Keller, Twitter.

Keith Keller, Global Twitter Marketing Specialist

E-mail

E-mail is, fundamentally, one of the oldest social networks and it's a private communications channel. I don't believe that everything you do

*needs to be public; not because I'm afraid for my privacy or anything
like that, but because I just want to make sure what I'm saying is
relevant to the right audience.*

Dennis Yu, Facebook expert and CEO of Blitz Local

I saved e-mail until last because it is often overlooked in terms of networking, but it is an essential tool in your armoury. Along with video calling and phone calls, e-mail is still a heavy hitter when it comes to building relationships. After all, as Dennis suggests, it is by far the most direct and simple way of keeping in touch, on a personal level, with your contacts. Close friends and colleagues are just a few keystrokes away from a conversation that is between just you and them and immediately feels personal. In today's broadcast world, these potentially quick personal interactions can keep you connected, and, ironically, because of the proliferation of spam, can be a stand-out message in your contact's inbox. Many people have moved on to even quicker forms of communication such as the instant messaging, texting and hangouts so a good old-fashioned e-mail that you have taken the time to craft is often appreciated.

How online and offline networking support each other

Many of our experts did not differentiate between their offline and online networking activities; instead highlighting the similarities of both environments *and* the symbiotic way that they supported each other.

Follow-up

The most obvious example of where the worlds of online and offline blur is in the area of follow-up:

- After a live meeting, you can follow up with that new contact by connecting with them online.
- After connecting with an individual online, you can follow up with a live meeting over coffee!

For many relationships though, it is the former of these scenarios that has transformed networking effectiveness. Following up now takes minutes rather than days and the quality of the follow-up can also be exponentially better as you have many resources at your disposal to share information, knowledge and connections.

Research

After follow-up, many of our experts highlighted research as being the next area where online supports offline effectively. The value they get by doing some background research on the people they are planning to meet is amazing.

> *I prepare myself by having a look at the participants' list which sometimes is available online or I'll just ask the organizers; and when I get the list I look up the people I want to meet online.*
>
> *I look in LinkedIn or I Google them and I find some background information about each and every one I want to talk to. When I get into a conversation with one of them I can bring into the conversation some of the things that I've researched. People are often impressed by how well that I prepared for that conversation and that helps us in getting to a deeper level at let's say a faster pace. Most people need two or three conversations to really get to the core and I'm able to speed that up and achieve that level with most people really in the first conversation.*
>
> Bert Verdonck, co-author of How to REALLY Use LinkedIn
> and Master Trainer at Really LinkedIn

Of course, research doesn't end there. Quite often, I have used the online tools to conduct research for my clients and taught others how to do it for their organization. The sheer volume of information written in these online tools is staggering and, importantly, easily searched. Keywords and good questions to your networks can elicit potential answers to your questions within minutes. In fact, 'Search' is fast becoming the next battleground as the likes of Facebook begin to challenge Google's pre-eminence in this area. As the functionality behind the networks converges, cross-platform searches will enable you to find not just material details but all of the related social interactions about those same facts too. It's one of the reasons why experts like Thomas Power encourage their clients to focus on consistency and transparency. They maintain that there is little point maintaining multiple profiles when the search engines can create composite pictures of you and all of your online activity with just a few keystrokes.

Online research is used most by the professionals in the recruitment industry. These days, job applicants need to ensure that their profiles on the major online platforms are as effective as their CV in promoting their value. Currently, LinkedIn is the main portal, but if a Search throws up some great material that you have posted on Facebook, Twitter or Google+ too, then you have just gained a potential jump on your competitors.

Introductions

I have now lost count of the number of people I have met at some live event or function and said, 'I'll introduce you to X when I get back online later.'

All of the online networking tools make it easy to introduce your connections to each other and this is by far one of the most important things you can do to help the people in your network as it expands and your influence grows. In fact, some people see it as the *most* important thing you can do for your network.

As our friend Yasmin Yellow says, be sure to give your connections 'an introduction to live up to'. Explain why you think this will be a good connection for both people and the value they have both brought to your life. As we're online, feel free to link to additional information about them that you think they will find interesting.

Keep in touch

Networking sites are not networking. They merely facilitate networking process. Networking process is building a network of people around you with whom you have a strong relationship, who you are happy to help and who are happy to help you.

Andy Lopata, best-selling author of Recommended: How to sell through networking and referrals *and leading business networking strategist*

Whether you make a new connection online or offline, one of the best things about online sites such as LinkedIn, Facebook, Google+ and Twitter is that they enable you to keep in touch with your connections incredibly easily. When I was younger, I met many people while travelling, studying or working and was keen to keep in touch, but it wasn't easy. Letters took time to write, postcards and their stamps were expensive and phone calls were difficult to organize with time differences a significant obstacle. Now, there are no excuses and instead a world of opportunities. We can add a new connection through a number of channels and, via updates, tagging and the occasional direct message, we can build and maintain that relationship easily. We can catch up live via Skype, we can share photographs and we can send humorous stories and jokes with just a few clicks. Obviously, the simple bit is the technical process, you still need to invest your time and emotion to strengthen relationships, but with the process simplified, we have time to do this more effectively. Experienced online relationship builders call this 'touching the nodes in the network' and just writing this piece has reminded me that I have an article that I need to share with two contacts – one in Arkansas and one in Cape Town. That will literally take me 30 seconds via e-mail and I might even post the same article in a LinkedIn group as it might spark some useful thinking for my contacts there.

Keep it simple. The important thing is to keep in touch with your connections. I go through my phone probably once or twice a month and anyone I haven't touched base with I might send a text or quick instant message just to see how things are going. There's nothing worse than where someone meets you, as an example; you hear nothing for 12 months and then they come to you and say, 'Oh, hi Lyndon. It's Simon. Can you do me a favour?' Why should I do you a favour? You haven't kept in touch. So it's important to keep in touch with your network.
Lyndon Wood, founder of SunZu (formerly Ecademy)

Key points

Being online is not about the technology – it is about the people. The technology is purely an enabler to help you find the right people and knowledge and ensure the right people find you.
Penny Power, author of Know Me, Like Me, Follow Me and co-founder of Ecademy

💬 Regardless of the tools you use, the key ingredient of networking remains the same, people. Like all tools, you can access greater levels of productivity and efficiency by deploying them effectively.

💬 How to build meaningful relationships with your online connections is our next topic to explore.

Building your reputation online

The way to gain a good reputation is to endeavour to be what you desire to appear.

Socrates

N ow that you have an overview of the key tools at your disposal for online networking, it's time to discuss how you approach your time online to achieve the most success. We've already identified 'building relationships' as the number one purpose for networking, so it won't surprise you to hear that your time online should also be focused on building relationships. For people to get to know you, to like you and what you're about and, ultimately, to trust you enough to recommend you, they need to feel like they have a solid relationship with you.

The three Cs

Your part in the process of building great relationships online is to be clear, to be consistent and to deploy the caring principle we discussed in Chapter 4. I'll summarize each of these at a high level first and then in more detail as we go through the rest of the chapter.

Clarity

Many online platforms have exactly the same constraints of e-mail:

- people don't devote enough time to finesse their written words;

- humour, emotion and sincerity are sometimes difficult to communicate; and

- the technology can get in the way (for example, chopping off important words or putting the send button too close to the save button).

Do your best to raise your awareness of these possibilities, and others, so that when you are communicating online, your message is getting through, *as intended*.

Another part of being clear is the impact and accessibility of your personal information. As your experience expands and your influence grows, the volume of achievements you could put into your online profiles could expand similarly. Focus on the key messages you want your network to know when they discover you or when they want to discuss you elsewhere. What are the top three things they might say about you? If you're not sure, ask a few friends what they would say about you, based on the key information you have put online. This is often very revealing. I was meeting a career coaching client of mine recently who was interested in switching jobs into a more strategic role, which was his real passion. However, when we looked at his profile on LinkedIn, it shrieked competent project manager. His mistake was assuming that potential employers would read all of the bullet points and discover his 'hidden talent' but really, most people have learned to scan information these days, fed by multi-channel, 24/7 media. What he needed was a headline that told everyone what he loved to do and then pick out all of the examples where he had done that successfully.

Consistency

If you are going to network in any environment, you'll have a distinct advantage if you are instantly recognized by your network contacts. So, think about using the same picture on all of the networks, and indeed the same key information. To take full advantage of the link-up between offline and online, it helps if your photo is relatively recent too; it helps people looking for you online and, vice versa, it enables them to spot you in a crowd if you are meeting up offline after striking up a conversation online.

Care

This is one area that the popular phrase 'fake it until you make it' just doesn't work. Even online, people can spot insincerity a mile off. Admittedly, there are times when you are too busy to respond as promptly or as fully as you would like, but generally people are willing to forgive this (unless it becomes the norm in your relationship with them). What we are discussing here is your genuine interest in the other person. Just like live networking, when you meet people online, take some time to find out about them, and the best way to do that is to ask some questions. Getting into the habit of asking yourself some enquiring questions about your new contacts will really boost your relationship with them. As you read their profile, ask yourself: What are they proud of? What or who inspires them? What are their likes/dislikes? Are they asking any questions online currently that you can answer?

All these little things can make a big difference to the development of your relationship, especially as picking up on these will demonstrate that you think they are worth researching.

Your Return on Reputation (ROR)

> *Don't judge each day by the harvest you reap, but by the seeds you plant.*
>
> Robert Louis Stevenson, novelist, poet,
> essayist, and travel writer

The prolific growth of social media and social networking sites in recent years, and the accelerating speed with which corporate entities are adopting new ways of engaging their key stakeholders means, for you, that if you are not managing your online presence then others may be doing it for you, and, even more likely, your competitors will be ahead of you! It is no accident that the most visible industry on LinkedIn is 'recruitment'. Recruiters spend hours researching their networks, seeking out candidates and analysing profiles. If you were in the market for a new job right now and they landed on your profile, or read your recent updates, would they be impressed?

> *In a networked, global economy, the old Return on Investment (ROI) model has evolved because now the major investment is in the time and effort it takes to build and maintain your Reputation in your Marketplace. So ROI has been replaced by ROR (Return On Reputation) – because it's the relationships you build up with your network that will yield a large proportion of your business. Your 'network' will include people you are connected to loosely, customers, ex-colleagues, current colleagues and everyone else who knows, likes, trusts and respects you and would recommend you – the model is as true for General Motors as it is for a freelance consultant.*
>
> Rory Murray, author of The Saw-Tooth Dilemma *and international business problem solver*

Your reputation is made up of many things and is built over time. It's the way you interact with others, the courtesy you extend to them, the way you talk about others (even when they can't hear you), it's the way you talk about yourself, it's the things you seek to share, it's your dominant thoughts and even what you find funny. All of these contribute to the perception others have of you. So, how should you approach this potential minefield? The watch-word is *mindfully*. You don't need to be someone that you are not. Instead, be the best you that you can be and be authentic. Perception is truth for the owner, and others will have a perception of you from your presence online anyway, so why not give them the best opportunity to see you at your best? As we discussed in Chapter 3, we are all capable of behaving in ways beyond our instinctive preferences, so take advantage of your ability to exhibit different energies if the situation calls for it. If you have a red preference and know that you can be perceived as abrupt sometimes, be mindful and add the odd nicety to a message. If your preference is yellow and you are in a flamboyant mood, but you sense your new contact is strongly blue, be mindful and keep it brief, to the point, and give them room to breathe. You get the idea. As you go beyond the introduction and start to build great relationships, the more this mindfulness (ie focus on the other person's needs) will become instinctive.

Like many things in life, the issue of building your reputation online is not necessarily complex. Your relationship with new network connections starts when they land on your profile or see you in a social media thread. Just like meeting in a room full of people, their perception of you will form almost instantly, so getting the basics right is the best place to start.

The basics

LinkedIn is arguably the most professional tool for networking online, so I thought the best people to help us understand how to get the basics right would be the LinkedIn experts themselves:

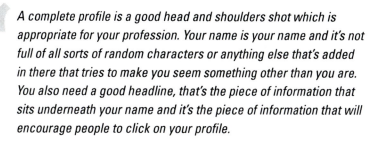

A complete profile is a good head and shoulders shot which is appropriate for your profession. Your name is your name and it's not full of all sorts of random characters or anything else that's added in there that tries to make you seem something other than you are. You also need a good headline, that's the piece of information that sits underneath your name and it's the piece of information that will encourage people to click on your profile.

It needs to contain keywords, because, of course, everything on LinkedIn is indexed. Just as Google indexes webpages, LinkedIn indexes and Google indexes LinkedIn as well. It's worth bearing that in mind.

Linda Parkinson-Hardman, author of LinkedIn Made Easy
and founder and CEO of The Hysterectomy Association

Applications are important. You can use for example a SlideShare presentation application so you can put PowerPoint presentations in there. But very important again, it's about building the know, like, trust

factor. People – sometimes they use applications to sell something, but it's too soon. The know, like, trust factor is not built yet.

Jan Vermeiren, co-author of How to REALLY Use LinkedIn

Far too many times, I see people's profiles on LinkedIn and they are full of boring stuff about work. They haven't included any of their personality, their style, the bits that make them them.

If you were to ask your clients why they engage with you, what it is that you do? Nine times out of ten it's the way you do things, not what you do.

The other thing with LinkedIn is just treat it like a big room of businesspeople. Use the same style or talk the same language. Act the same way. Stop trying to treat it like it's something different.

James Potter, 'The LinkedIn Man' – strategic business adviser

Returning briefly to your photo, you just need to ask yourself one question: 'Why is it there?' The answer, very clearly, is so that people can get a first impression of you. You don't have the luxury of a handshake, a warm greeting or a nice introduction by someone else; it's just your picture, so make it recognizable and representative. There is no absolute formula or even industry standards, just take a look around and see what sort of pictures grab your attention in your area of expertise. You don't need to try too hard to be unique, your face is designed that way already.

Beyond grabbing the attention of your readers, your profile serves two further purposes: to introduce you to others in the network and to provide your readers with reasons to connect. One of the first social business networks online was Ecademy and your profile there had space for 50 words that meant something to you. The recommendation was to make it about 50 per cent business and 50 per cent personal and it worked a treat. The most popular word that triggered connections for me on my profile was 'rhubarb'. I love rhubarb and I have been known to travel many a mile with the promise of a bowl of rhubarb crumble and custard (or cream, or ice-cream, or all three!). The value of this sort of simple disclosure is that it breaks the ice and gives the person making contact an easy way to connect – even if it is to say how much they hate rhubarb! What you are doing is lowering the threshold for people to connect with you, which is, after all, the purpose of networking in the first place!

Once you have set up your profile, the remaining basics will vary depending on which platform you are using to build your network relationships. Wherever you are though, just keep thinking about making connections, contributing knowledge and sharing resources.

Be professional

When Facebook and LinkedIn first became popular, you would often hear people say things like: 'I use Facebook for my friends and family and LinkedIn for business.' The assumption was that they could 'be' different people with different networks – more relaxed on Facebook for example. However, it is becoming increasingly obvious that the ability for you to present two different images of yourself online is not sustainable. The constant erosion of personal privacy once you venture online is significant.

Online, the opportunities to be less than professional are increasing all the time; from posting rude videos on YouTube through to saying something hurtful on someone's Facebook wall. Regardless of the provocation, the only thing an external observer will see is what *you* have done; and, when it comes to recruiting someone or choosing a supplier, the margins can be very slim at the decision point. The slightest indiscretion can create an unfavourable perception of you that might just swing against you. Perception, as they say, is reality.

A great rule of thumb when it comes to judging how to interact with people online is to ask yourself, 'What would I say if I was sitting next to them?' This will achieve two things: first, you will write more fluently and your 'voice' will come through very clearly; and second, you are likely to be 'courteous enough' to maintain the relationship you have with your correspondent.

This may sound like a curious way of phrasing it, but there are social networks on which it has become popular to engage in conversations that you would be unlikely to overhear if those involved were physically sat next to each other. Similarly, I am always disappointed when people add crude and vulgar remarks and personal slights to the threads on open forums. Ignoring the impact on a fellow human being for a moment, it is almost as if they have completely forgotten that they are not alone with their laptop, tablet or phone; they are, in fact, communicating to a potential global audience. If you do feel the urge to write something that you sense you may regret later, here's a great tip:

> *Never, ever, post anything on social media in anger. I have a little – well, in fact, it's a rather large Word document and it's called 'The Blog I Can't Publish' and every time I want to have a really good rant, I go and I type it up in that document and I feel like I've kind of released myself from it, but I know I can't possibly publish it.*
>
> Dinah Liversidge, co-founder of #thebreakfastclub
>
> and *Executive Business Mentor*

To further emphasize the point, here are three stories that I read about this week that highlight what I am talking about:

1   The first is of a young man who decided to have some fun at work. He worked in the warehouse attached to a large supermarket and, in a fit of youthful exuberance, he decided to take a bunch of photos of himself fooling around and posing in various states of undress. His mistake was to upload the photos to Facebook and share them with his friends. The photos were seen by his manager and, to cut a long story short, he lost his job.

2   The second is of a young professional who filmed a practical joke and put it on YouTube, complete with identifying commentary. Two days later, the police were at her door threatening to charge her with a minor offence. Similar cases have resulted in criminal charges and the social networks have become a good source of police intelligence.

3   Finally, a third young man from the UK, found himself the subject of a lengthy interrogation at US airport security before being expelled from the country, all because of a tweet he'd posted using a slang expression for 'having a party'. He said he was looking forward to his trip to 'destroy America'. Unfortunately, this message was picked up by US Homeland Security who were at first alarmed by the message and then unwilling to accept the story behind it. He was detained at the US airport and returned home on the next available flight.

I don't relay these stories to advocate any specific form of behaviour – you need to make your own mind up on that one; all I am doing is highlighting the issues that permanent visibility of the information you post are creating. If you would rather not have the reputation that comes with such behaviour, you know what to do!

What the online gurus say and do

" *The thing with online is that, everything that happens offline, happens online as well, only faster.*

William Buist, collaboration specialist, director at Abelard Management Services Limited

As I mentioned in the previous chapter, you can enhance your professional reputation both online and offline by working effectively online, especially LinkedIn. Make each time you are on LinkedIn count. Don't just browse around or review the jobs, work your network. Who can you help? Who has a question that you can either answer or refer them to someone that can? Do you have a question of your own?

Make sure that you are using LinkedIn Answers. It's one of the easiest and fastest ways to gather expertise and a broader network. But only answer questions or only post questions where you A, genuinely have something of use to offer the conversation, that is going to be of interest or B, that it's something that you genuinely want to know. There are far too many spammers using these facilities and what you don't want to do is to be tarred with the same brush.

Linda Parkinson-Hardman, author of LinkedIn Made Easy *and founder and CEO of The Hysterectomy Association*

Someone told me that you are the average of the five people you spend the most time with. So what area do you want to be known for? I will ask people, 'What is your area of expertise? What are you world class in?' Based on that, who are the five people that you need to spend time with? Maybe you don't feel that you operate in their arena yet. But who are those five people? Reach out and say hi. Subscribe to them. Put 'like' on their comments. Read their articles. Try to find some way to comment back and say something and pretty soon, you will build a relationship with these folks and it's amazing how accessible a lot of these folks are. For example, I wanted to talk about Facebook, so I met Mark Zuckerberg a couple of times. I didn't stalk him. He reached out to

me because of the content that I produce. I think the key is just A, reach out to those people with something meaningful and B, produce content that demonstrates you're an expert.

Dennis Yu, Facebook expert and CEO of Blitz Local

CASE STUDY   The five S's

Rob Brown is one of the most knowledgeable people in the world about networking. I was first introduced to Rob when he was looking for interviewees for a series of conversations to help his clients in the banking sector to be better managers and leaders. At that time, we were talking about mastering time but when I caught up with him recently, it was my turn to ask the questions. His response to the question, 'What are your five top tips for networking online?' was among the highlights. Over to Rob:

1 Sticky profile – something that stands out just a little bit. By sticky, I mean it makes people want to stick around. There are too many profiles that are bland. Gary Hamel has a lovely two-word quote that says simply, 'Sameness sucks.' All of my work is around personal marketing and getting people to come to you first above and beyond all of their other choices. You know, those promo-phobic people that are not good at selling themselves and let's face it, we're all selling. So first up, get a sticky profile and that might mean getting photos on there or something personal about you.

2 Be strategic – decide in advance the kind of people you want to meet. If you can get a target market, that's great. But be very strategic about who you spend your time with because time is precious.

3 Say no – take some time to calibrate your relationships and get rid of some and make some space in the closet to bring in some new clothes, if you like. The Pareto principle of 80–20 (named after Italian economist, Vilfredo Pareto), indicates that 20 per cent of the relationships you have will yield you 80 per cent of your results. So let's focus more on those people and there are lots of tools and software and systems to help you do that. So definitely 'say no!'

4 Skill up – put simply, work on your networking skills. Learn how to remember names. Teach yourself to type. Master the networking tools at your disposal.

Become familiar with Facebook and LinkedIn. Working on your skills and knowledge is a fabulous way to raise your game.

5   Sell yourself – selling yourself is a very underrated and very overlooked talent these days. People say, 'If I'm good enough', but you can't survive in this economic climate by being ordinary. So you've got to sell yourself. This means any kind of ethical bragging and let's remind ourselves that it was Muhammad Ali that said, 'It isn't bragging if you've done it.' So putting yourself up, sharing stories about yourself, giving examples about how you solved problems, and the differences you've made with people. Make that your elevator pitch, not your job title or your benefit statement, but examples of stuff that you've done, evidence for your supremacy. Sell yourself and we're all selling. You might not be selling products and services but everyone is selling a vision, an idea, an argument, an excuse, an opinion, a proposition. We're selling projects. We're selling leadership. We're selling ourselves. The biggest sell we've got to make every single day of our lives is selling those to ourselves, selling you to you. You've got to look yourself in the mirror every single day and say, 'This is what I do. I'm really good at it and the price is X. To be honest Mr Prospect, that's really good value for you because you get me.' How often can you see with people that they don't make that first sale to themselves? They're just not sure about themselves. They don't back themselves. They're not confident enough in their own proposition and people buy certainty. Certainty is referable. Certainty is compelling and attractive

ROB BROWN!

I ♥ NOTWORKING

and if you're certain and sure of yourself, that's attractive. That's magnetic. That's compelling and that will get people wanting to meet you and talk about you and recommend and refer you. So get in a frame of mind where you're selling yourself comfortably because that's the one thing that's going to make all your networking click into place.

Rob Brown, best-selling author of How to Build Your Reputation
and Head of the Global Networking Council

Key points

It takes 20 years to build a reputation and five minutes to ruin it. If you think about that, you'll do things differently.

Warren Buffet, investor and philanthropist

Online, your network can read about you, see you in action and hear what you have to say – 24/7. It has never been so easy to demonstrate your value and indeed your values.

In the next chapter, we will look at how you can deploy all of this networking knowledge and skill in the workplace.

How to network effectively at work

When you tug at a single thing in nature, you find it attached to the rest of the world.

John Muir, pioneering naturalist

Forget the world for a moment, but recognize the power of that quote when it comes to the world of work. Every person you meet in work is very obviously connected to someone else in the organization. Naturally, some are more connected than others and we'll come back to them later. For now, just appreciate that everyone is connected… and so are you. In fact, your network experiences a positive step change as soon as you start work and throughout your career you should pay close attention to it, building it all the time. It is so important that it has led some commentators to say: 'Your network will determine your net worth.'

Starter for 10

Let's start by having a look at who you will meet automatically and how you may want to think about them in terms of networking. I'm going to take them in the chronological order that you may meet them.

The receptionist

In my humble opinion, the receptionists are the unsung heroes of most businesses and they are usually at the top of my list of favourite people in almost every organization that I've ever been. Who else can welcome everyone with a smile, sort out all of the administrative details associated with visitors and service personnel, know where almost everyone is in the business and talk to half a dozen different people while ensuring that you proceed to your destination quickly and safely?

If it's your first day, say 'Hello' and introduce yourself as the new person starting in the X department. I can guarantee, you will not only get a personal welcome on your second day but you'll have made your first friend. The receptionist is a bit like the host at a live networking event; they can direct you effectively, give you advanced notice of things to watch out for and even introduce you to some other people that you may want to meet.

The HR department

HR stands for human resources and, guess what? They know a few people! However, like everyone else that you meet, it's not about what they can do for you but how you can help each other. In modern organizations, HR have an unenviable job; not only are they responsible for welcoming people into the organization but also, metaphorically, escorting them off the premises at the end of their stay – not to mention, looking after them at all stages in between. You can make their job easier by having everything with you that you are requested to bring when you start your new job. This will leave you more time to start building a relationship.

The better the people in the HR team know you, the more likely it is that they will keep in touch and check how you are settling in. Very often they will be more aware than your new team of things that are going on across the business and will be your best route into other departments.

Your boss

In my career I have interviewed, trained, coached, mentored and worked alongside thousands of bosses; from first line managers right up to chief executives and almost all of them have had at least a slight concern over their ability to get everything done that they knew needed to be done. All had developed strategies to improve their personal effectiveness but the higher up in the organization their career progressed, the more effective they were at achieving results through the deployment of other people. As you join their team, your job is to find out the main things that your boss is hoping to achieve and then quickly align your activity to support them in that mission.

Your new boss may, or may not, be the best networker in your office but you can guarantee that they are still connected to a lot of people. It is very easy to think that your only job when you start in a team is to do whatever your boss requests of you, but you would be wrong. Whether you have just joined as the new finance director or the apprentice book-keeper, in addition to your 'day job', it is essential that you start to build relationships across the organization… just in case. 'Just in case of what?' I hear you ask. Well, just in case an issue arises that cannot be resolved inside the team. You don't know what those issues might be or when they might occur, but if you are the one who is able to tap into your network and find a suitable solution, you have just transformed into the MVP (most valuable person) in your boss's team. This is not about being an obnoxious creep who only does things to court the boss's favour; this is about recognizing the professional value in being connected across the organization, no matter what level you are working at today.

Your colleagues

In the good old days, I would have used the term 'team' rather than colleagues, but in these days of matrixed organizations, flexible workers and individuals with multiple roles, it is more accurate to think outside of the tight confines of a team when it comes to who you might meet next inside your new organization.

On my first day at Andersen Consulting (now Accenture), I was sat behind someone who I really didn't think I wanted to get to know at all. It was January 1992 and this was the first day of my new professional career. His name was Rahul and I had mistaken his quirky sense of humour for arrogance. It was a full three days before I finally realized that underneath his façade of bravado was the most wonderful and generous human being. We quickly became firm friends and I am pleased to say that I can still call him today to announce that I'm in town and I'll receive the most amazing welcome from his whole family, especially his mum, whose southern Indian cooking is simply out of this world.

The immediate colleagues you meet will provide your initial route into the organization, so get to know them well and always seek to add value to their lives. Remember some funny or uplifting stories to tell them, remember birthdays, keep up to date with any news that they share with you; whether that be football or the birth of their first nephew – if it's important to them, then you have just been offered a point of connection. Of course, you may not fit this particular profile, your style may be less engaging or outgoing. However, think about what you do well with people – it could be humour, or dependability, or even thoughtfulness; whatever it is, bring it to work with you every day and share it with your colleagues.

The cleaner

If you are wondering why the cleaner is in this list, then you haven't been paying attention. No-one in this list is the title we have given them. Your boss feeds the dog at home, your colleagues watch the football on TV and the cleaner probably runs marathons to raise money for the local hospice. The other thing that they do is possess the keys to the building should you get locked in late at night!

Glass ceilings

To be successful at anything, there needs to be a lot of other people that want you to be successful. 'No man is an island' is a phrase I grew up with. John Donne wrote these words nearly 400 years ago, but they are more pertinent today than they have ever been. We lead increasingly connected lives and the sooner we realize the truth in this matter, the easier life becomes. We are all interdependent. We may think we live independent lives, especially if we live away from our families, but the reality is we depend entirely on our community for our health, wealth and mobility. Our ability to grow and prosper is intricately linked to the mindset and behaviours of others, and nowhere more so than in work. It is undoubtedly true that we need to have self-belief and the courage of our convictions, but if we are to be successful in work, then our ability to get on with people is critical.

As a career mentor, I have often worked with people that are experiencing the 'glass ceiling' effect and feel stuck. Their careers have not progressed as they had hoped and they are constantly overlooked when it comes to promotions. Sometimes this can be completely baffling to the individual concerned and can even come down to prejudice. In fact, the phrase 'glass ceiling' is almost synonymous with the, frankly, ridiculous practice of systemically favouring men over their female colleagues when it comes to promotion. Thankfully, this happens far less now than was the case in the past, primarily due to the attitude of women like Madeleine Albright:

I love being a woman and I was not one of these women who rose through professional life by wearing men's clothes or looking masculine. I loved wearing bright colors and being who I am.
Madeleine Albright, first woman to become the US Secretary of State

Returning though to the more generic instances of glass ceilings, it is the nature of organizations that, to get things done, we will need to work with others and therefore, our success will always be influenced by the impression others have of us, both our colleagues and our bosses. Depending on your level, and function, inside the organization, you may be able to stay 'under the radar' but, as a general rule, the higher up you go, the more you will need to have developed solid relationships and have effective internal networks. In essence, the more strategic your role, or the more dependencies with other departments, the better your network will need to be.

Given this, part of your ability to be promoted will be determined by how well your employers think you will fit with the existing team and how effective they presume you will be at getting results through and with others. You can be a very nice person, you can be more than technically competent and you can even have some great ideas, but at the end of the day, if people still don't know you, then they will never have the opportunity to see if they like or trust you and will therefore not be in a position to recommend you for promotion when the time comes. Quite often, glass ceilings are merely an indication that you need to develop better relationships with your co-workers so that they can perceive your value. The reality is that we are all busy and other people are not going to go out of their way to find out about what you do to see if they can help you. You need to spread the word yourself, become your own PR consultant for Me Inc. Sing your own praises occasionally but make sure it is backed up with solid deeds.

Leadership is a measure of influence

True leadership cannot be awarded, appointed, or assigned. It comes only from influence, and that cannot be mandated. It must be earned.
John Maxwell, internationally recognized leadership expert, speaker, coach and author

John Maxwell is a world authority on leadership and I highly recommend his books if you'd like to find out more. He supports this point about leadership with six factors that make a leader, and one of those is relationships. If you have aspirations of leading people at work, then you need to develop deep relationships with the key people that can influence your progress. Of course, you understand already the value in developing a wide network but supplementing that with a strategic approach can reap big rewards. The first thing you need to do is identify who are the key influencers in any given department. If you can identify these individuals, then you have just developed a short-cut into that part of the organization and increased your chances of getting to know how that area works and how you may be able to contribute to their success. This approach is similar to a process called stakeholder mapping, which project managers employ to determine how they can influence and support the key people that will be either directly or indirectly affected by the change that their project will bring about. Among other things, a good project manager will want to understand the influence and power of each stakeholder as well as how they feel about the project. The purpose of the analysis is to determine how they can seek to influence them positively. Similarly, you can map out the key people that you want to get to know inside your organization and think about how you are going to build a relationship with them to extend your influence.

Just as a gentle reminder though, focus more on the relationship than your desired outcome. In fact, once you have decided that you would like to extend your influence inside the company, you can almost take your eyes off your key stakeholders and revert to the general strategy of befriending everyone you meet. Ultimately, having any motive other than it is good to get to know your colleagues will prevent you from building authentic relationships. Let things develop naturally and just be yourself.

So, let's summarize what we have discussed so far in this section on networking at work. Just like every other aspect of your networking, the focus is always on just making friends and the quickest way to do that is to be genuinely interested in them. In fact, you can do even better than that, learn to be fascinated by the people you meet. Be ultra-curious. Don't worry, it is highly unlikely that your curiosity will be over the top, but try not to ask lots of quick-fire questions because that can be off-putting. Remember too that when building relationships, the focus is the other person: how can you help them? Are there resources you can share? Introductions you can make?

Finally, a note to those of you who are specifically taking on a new job at a senior level – get out from behind your desk and meet people where they are. Our next case study features someone who is superb at this. Small wonder that Jerry is so sought after in his industry!

CASE STUDY

I met Jerry Hopkins on our first day at Barry Boys Comprehensive School in 1979. We were both in Class 1J, Jerry was No 10 on the register and I was No 17 with only John, Jones, Mahoney, Mason, Owens and Passey between us! (I know, very sad that I remember, but we did hear the register called out twice a day for two years.) Jerry had an easy style about him even then, made friends effortlessly. His quick humour and natural ability to build rapport with people enabled him to develop friendships with both school mates and teachers alike. Jerry had learned very early in life that people are just people and they won't bite if you talk to them. In fact, talking did seem to be his favourite subject, regardless of which teacher was stood at the front of the class! Just kidding Jerry.

We went our separate ways when it was time to go to university but reconnected again about 10 years ago. In the interim, Jerry had made a big impact with a few different companies and was consistently promoted to look after bigger and bigger teams or boost performance in areas where the real issue was not technology or process, but people. Over the course of a few years and many conversations (usually as we were heading in separate directions on Britain's motorway network), it became clear to me that Jerry had mastered the art of networking at work, so when I knew I was going to be writing this book, he was the first person I spoke to for this particular chapter.

Jerry is brilliant at recognizing the value of meeting people where they are in the business. He shunned an office in favour of an open plan desk in his most recent appointment as operations director and, in his first few days, he made a point of not being at his desk at all. Instead, he was out meeting the guys in the warehouse, helping them shift stock and just chatting to them. Finding out all about them and being curious, being fascinated. This practice is often cited in good management books; it's even got a label 'managing by walking the floor', and there are indeed many benefits, from an operational perspective, of walking among your fellow workers to learn all about the business. However, this is not Jerry's primary reason for walking around. First and foremost, Jerry is seeking to make new friends in his new workplace. He is building relationships; and to do that, he needs to find out a lot about them: What motivates them? What annoys them? What sports team do they follow? Slowly, he builds a network that spreads across the whole organization and he knows as much as anyone about the people that make it work!

When I caught up with Jerry, I asked him for a few of his top tips. Here's what he said:

> *I'm not sure I every really had a strategy, but the three things that I have done consistently across my career are:*

- *Spend time with your people who are actually doing the job – day in, day out. Listen and absorb what they're saying. Let them teach you what they're doing, regardless of their job title. It's about a half-mile walk around the warehouse and I do that two or three times a day with one or two of the store managers.*

- *Have an energy about yourself. You need to keep yourself fit and have bags of energy. People with bags of energy are able to not only get their own job done but pass that energy onto others and people are always pleased to see them.*

- *Stay in touch with people – both socially and business-wise. I think it's important to keep in touch with all of your colleagues and friends.*

> *Jerry Hopkins, Operations Director for Williams Medical Supplies*

Influence your industry

Talking of industry, let's turn our attention now to the space beyond your place of work. How do you extend your influence outside the organizational chart and across your industry? Well, these days, it is considerably easier than it used to be. In the old days, it may have taken you a whole career to gain a reputation in your industry, or else the development of a service or tool that was extraordinary or perhaps a piece of timely luck. In general though, people stayed with the same company throughout their whole career and mobility was limited. You might become well known within your company, but it was the company that took the headlines when something significant happened.

These days, due to the preponderance of 24-hour media, online and print journalism and, most importantly, social media, the focus has switched to individuals and not always just when there is bad news to broadcast. Services such as LinkedIn and Twitter make it easy for an individual to let the whole world know when they have been involved in something significant. If their company has just launched a new product and they were heavily involved in its production, they can stake their claim immediately. Similarly, if they have written an industry report, they can identify themselves as authors even if the intellectual property belongs to their employer.

Why bother? Well, lifelong careers are few and far between, so strategic management of your career is important and extending your influence in your industry of choice is a wise move. So, as well as finding ways to increase your exposure, think about the following networking tips for building your reputation.

What have you got to say?

Regardless of what industry you are in, there will be some aspects that either annoy you or make you want to sing. Identify them and then start talking about them. Do some research, gather some facts and interesting statistics. Develop your own considered opinion and then think about how you can share that within your network and beyond into the industry as a whole. Get into groups on LinkedIn and share your opinions through providing answers to other people's questions. Pretty soon you will have a reputation as someone who is not only helpful, but has something interesting to say too.

Look for peers

Peers are people at your level or similar, potentially in the same function but not exclusively. Importantly, you are not seeking to network with them for competitive reasons. Knowing who your peers are and inviting them into your network is not so that you can work out their weaknesses, it is actually so that you can support each other. They will be facing similar challenges to you, at similar times, and having an independent adviser on-hand to give you some objective guidance is invaluable. Invariably, you will find that you bump into the same people again and again at different times in your career, as you move from one organization to another. Imagine how useful it is to start in a new business and know several of the key people in the organization already? Within your online networks, peer relationships can be vital when it comes to finding that next role or spreading the word when you have something significant to say.

Link up and meet up

There really is no excuse these days when it comes to being able to identify and build relationships with people that you want in your network. The multiple online platforms mean that you can find almost anyone. Send them an invitation to link up and then, as soon as you can, see if you can meet up – either online with a video conference or live if possible. I was lucky enough to attend the school of online social business networking, otherwise known as Ecademy. The founders, Thomas and Penny Power were brilliant at helping people make great connections through balancing online interaction and offline one-to-ones. A one-to-one, as the name implies, is simply a face-to-face meeting, usually over coffee with the intention of doing nothing more than getting to know the other person better. For many years I was part of the group of networkers on Ecademy called BlackStar and through that group, I managed to eliminate my marketing budget. Through what I learned with that group and the relationships I formed within it, I created more than enough work to keep me going. I also made some friends that will stay with me for life and you will find a number of them in between the pages of this book. We all learned a lot together and continue to support each other to this day – some through the successor to Ecademy, Lyndon Woods's SunZu, some through Fraser Hay's Grow Your Business Club, some through Warren Cass's Business Scene and still others through Dave Clarke's NRG Networks. The combination of social and business is potent – never underestimate it.

Conferences, talks and papers

The final recommendation when it comes to building your reputation in your industry is to consider the multitude of great opportunities to become an authority. Again, the growth of online tools has been revolutionary. Blogging is an increasingly popular way to build an audience for your thoughts. Along with tools such as Slide Share, Camtasia and Videos you can be literally minutes away from promoting yourself to the world. Recently, I observed a video go viral on Facebook, propelling the responsible individual into the limelight on an issue of which he had no previous experience. It was a sparse piece of video, as he talked into the camera of his phone and proceeded to share an emotional message about a film he had just watched. Within hours the comments numbered in their hundreds and his video was shared across the world. It led to some interesting opportunities and a certain celebrity status almost overnight. If he can do that for an issue that was nothing to do with his industry, imagine what you can do, armed with all of your knowledge? Those people you see on stage at conferences, giving talks at local events and publishing papers are just like you. Every single one of them had to do it for a first time, once. Start small, go to a local Toastmasters meeting or volunteer to give a talk at work to a few of your colleagues at the next meeting. From there, use your network to seek out people that are running events and just ask if they need someone to talk on your topic – you'll be surprised at just how many will be more than pleased you asked. The volume of events taking place every day in every city and town is unbelievable and most want to entertain and educate their audience, so step right up and shine!

Landing a job

For most professionals, LinkedIn is the first port of call when it comes to researching and finding the next job. It's not the only tool in the box but it is fair to say that most industries are represented on there.

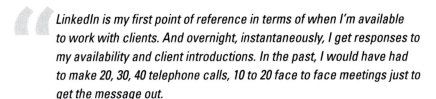

*LinkedIn is my first point of reference in terms of when I'm available
to work with clients. And overnight, instantaneously, I get responses to
my availability and client introductions. In the past, I would have had
to make 20, 30, 40 telephone calls, 10 to 20 face to face meetings just to
get the message out.*

Damon Lawrenson, award-winning interim Financial Director

If you don't have great networks in your line of work, you may find the process of landing your next job extremely frustrating. The phrase, 'don't dig your well when you are thirsty' is very relevant here. However, if you have put in the groundwork and built your networks over time and expanded into your industry, building an enviable reputation, when you are looking for work, you will find your network will come to you. Some people in your network will have been waiting for you to become available, your reputation is so strong!

It is far better to be on that side of the fence than on the other side realizing that many of the jobs you want are not even advertised, they are sourced through the networks of the people doing the hiring. Even the advertised jobs will have certain candidates in waiting, tipped off again by the hiring individual in their network. Is it right? Maybe not. Is it human behaviour? Absolutely. Who knows, likes, trusts and refers you? Do you know? When was the last time you made contact? Go on, what are you waiting for?

Key points

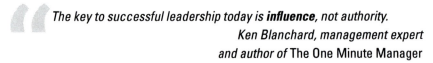

*The key to successful leadership today is **influence**, not authority.*
*Ken Blanchard, management expert
and author of* The One Minute Manager

● Networking at work is all about expanding your zone of influence, both through your own activities and through the alignment of your activities with the aspirations of other key individuals across the organization or industry.

● In the next chapter we will begin to measure our performance in this world of networking, using the networking scorecard.

The networking scorecard

Not everything that can be counted counts, and not everything that counts can be counted.

Albert Einstein, theoretical physicist and developer of the general theory of relativity

So, you've got a goal, you've even got a five-step implementation plan, do you need anything else? Yes you do – you need to measure your progress and success, otherwise, networking will become another bucket for lost time in your business or your life. Measurement transforms networking from an activity that you feel you ought to be doing into a powerful strategic tool. However, this chapter comes with two words of warning – networker beware! Can you really put a value on a relationship? If you construct a networking strategy for your project or your business, can you really maintain the highest levels of authenticity and truly be there for the other people that you meet? Well, the answer is yes – if you remember that you are not judging the individuals or indeed the specific setting in which you encounter them. Your aim with measurement is to be a better networker and to measure your own effectiveness. How well did you listen? How well did you follow up? What value did you add?

A professional approach

I presented my description of a professional in Chapter 6, Building your reputation online, but it is worth reiterating at this stage. A professional networker is someone who does what they say they will do, with good grace and always with the other person's interests at heart.

One thing a professional always strives to do is raise the level of confidence they have both personally, and as perceived by the people around them, in their actions, usually through the delivery of results. In the area of networking, you will boost your self-confidence immensely if you are able to capture the results you achieve. What has the time and money you have invested in networking returned for you and by what measure? Essentially, what we are trying to get at is '*why*' we measure, and there are many reasons:

What gets measured gets done

The networking scorecard delivers one critically important factor to your networking – FOCUS. Using a scorecard to monitor your progress towards your networking goals, you will have an immediate, and simple, reminder of the most important aspects of networking that you can reference at any point. The list of benefits this will deliver for you is substantial:

- Over time, you can see how effective certain networking events, platforms and activities are in terms of contribution to your specific goals.
- You'll have a written record of who you need to follow up.
- Your database can be maintained effortlessly.
- You will regain control of your diary as you schedule in follow-up meetings and calls.
- Data can be shared within teams enabling proactive follow-ups as required.
- Connections can be made more easily, increasing your value to your network.
- It will also help you to say 'no' to networking opportunities that are not appropriate for you right now.

What you are doing here is improving your effectiveness as a networker. You are not turning your network into a set of numbers. Remember, every person you meet is an individual with aspirations, goals, wants and needs just like you and by capturing your verbal commitments, you are merely demonstrating that you care about them. Unless you are a world-beating memory champion, there is every possibility that life may just get in the way, between the point when you agree to help someone and the time when you will have an opportunity to fulfil that commitment, so help yourself and write it down!

Networking is not free...

...or even low cost!

There are many costs associated with networking, from the travel costs for live events to the opportunity costs when your time online could be invested in other activities. I know many small business owners who invest several thousands of pounds each year attending live meetings; the money spent on fuel, food and fizz needs to be accounted for, along with the amount of time you spend travelling and at the event itself. So, capturing the cost and time spent for each activity will help you understand what resources you are committing to your networking. The same can be said for time spent online, networking on the social business platforms; whether that is time spent updating your own information, time spent responding to queries and requests or the time you spend building relationships – it all adds up!

Measuring value

Once you know how much of your precious time and resources you are investing in your networking efforts, you can start to gauge the 'value' of each network in terms of contribution towards your life and business goals, but, as I mentioned earlier, be careful how you measure.

CASE STUDY

Bill was in month three of his new business and, by his own admission, he had become a bit of networking junkie. He had joined two local networking groups, was a member of three business support groups that held their own events and had also set up profiles on Facebook and LinkedIn. The result was he spent many hours each week travelling to meetings or joining others in online groups, sharing great information and helping others when he could. The problem was, to date, he had received no business through his networks.

When I met him, he was on the verge of withdrawing from almost everything and moaning about his inability to afford an industry conference that he knew would put him in front of several hundred prospects.

However, when we looked at how his network was really developing and assessed it using some of the metrics discussed in this chapter, he gained an entirely different perspective. In three short months, he had acquired connections to individuals inside four target clients and many more prospects. Admittedly, none of these were buyers but two of them were in a position to introduce him directly, if he spent some time cultivating the relationships.

Effectively, Bill was generalizing – 'networking is not working for me and my business', when in reality, it was only *some* of his networking activity that was not delivering. Of course, any activity where you are engaging with other people can lead to a prospect for your business eventually, but when cash flow is tight and time is more critical, you need to make some tough choices and focus on the parts of your network that are demonstrably delivering results now!

Together, we drafted a second 90-day plan for Bill, which focused on just one local networking group, nurturing the relationships with existing leads, following up on great prospects and registering for the industry conference. All other events were cancelled to free up time and, of course, cash, to prepare for the conference which was a significant success. Not as significant as the results delivered by Bill's new network though. By focusing on relationships and determining real needs, Bill was passed several lucrative connections. In fact, in terms of business generation, the network outstripped the conference by three to one.

Systemize – *working* on *your network*

Those of you familiar with Michael Gerber's 'e-myth', will be aware of the phrase, 'work *on* your business not in your business'. Gerber is passionate about the inherent value in systemizing your business. In the context of small- and medium-sized businesses, networking can deliver great results and replace spend on traditional activities such as marketing and PR. Doesn't it make sense then to systemize your networking? Capturing how you decide where to network, your approach to networking, the costs associated with each aspect of your networking as well as the essential data for the relationships you build, makes it easy for other people in your business to duplicate what you do. Duplication is critical if you have aspirations of growing your business beyond yourself. The same is true in the context of a project, if, as a team, you can share the information on your growing network of stakeholders, each person that the project touches will feel that much more engaged with what is happening and how they can help.

Luckily, systemizing your networking is not a difficult task. In fact, there are two simple steps that, if you take them weekly, will have it all done in no time: 1) review your weekly networking actions, as captured in your networking scorecards; and 2) plan your next actions.

Serial entrepreneur, Nigel Botterill talks about investing '90 minutes' at the start of every day to work on the most important aspect of your business if you want it to grow – marketing. And, as networking is a great way to market your business, why not take up one of these slots every week to work *on* your network. What's working for you? What can you improve? Where does your network need nurturing? Who can you help? These reviews will be even easier if you keep everything graphical. Make it a habit to draw out parts of your network, such as the network map of key stakeholders in your project, and pin it up. Make sure the task of maintaining your network stays on your to-do list too, until it becomes a routine.

Keep it personal

It is very easy when we're discussing 'networks', 'stakeholders' and 'prospects' to forget that behind everything are people just like you and me. Personally, I have the opposite problem; I find it difficult to see beyond the individuals and see the networks sometimes. Fundamentally, we are always talking about relationships. Every expert that I interviewed said exactly the same thing; treating people as 'contacts', 'connections' or 'groups' will destroy your credibility and undermine every relationship you have. When you are measuring the effectiveness of your networking, you are not measuring any one or any group of individuals, you are merely assessing where you can apply your time most effectively, so that you can become, in the long term, an effective member of your networks. If you build great relationships, you will naturally expand your influence, generate more value for your business/ family/community and be in a position to help others even more.

So, when you are networking, invest your time and energy in others first. Be personable, help, make introductions, contribute your thoughts, share your knowledge and expertise and take a personal interest in their lives. Take the view that, one day, all of your best connections will be, not just your friends, but your closest companions on life's journey. It doesn't matter if that is not the way it transpires, just set off with that intent. Some friends will wander off in different directions to you but others will share a longer trip. The fun part is seeing who is still there many years after you met them. In my case, many of the long-standing friends seem to be united only in one feature – their inability to shake me off!

The right metrics

My golden rule of networking is simple: don't keep score.
Harvey Mackay, author of Swimming with Sharks

So, if counting the number of business cards you collected at the latest conference or breakfast meeting is not a great measure for determining your effectiveness as a networker, what are the right measures to track? Let's start with the end in mind... you want to become an effective networker and, as we will discover in Chapter 9, the complete professional networker is organized, supportive and a great connector; so it makes sense to design a scorecard that is going to help you focus on those attributes. It is also worth recognizing here the relationship between offline and online networking and how the two can also work for you independently. For example, many of our experts talked of how they supplemented their live events with online preparation and follow up, in the ways we discussed in the five-step plan, but others highlighted the opportunity to develop relationships completely online, especially when the connection has come through a trusted source. There is usually still a desire to meet up face to face when you have made a fantastic connection online, but it is not essential for a great working relationship to develop.

Offline

Your focus at live events then is not on selling, it's not on how much food and drink you can consume and most definitely not on handing out as many cards as you can. Instead, your focus is on making new friends and building existing relationships. These are therefore the drivers of the main metrics you record.

When you meet someone new, whether that is at a networking event, an industry conference or a project meeting, the key things you want to find out are:

 name;
role;

contact details (e-mail, mobile number and social media names); and

 what are they working on right now?

At a business networking event, the last of these *may* lead on to a conversation in which they reveal who would be a great referral for them right now, but don't always make this assumption. In fact, depending on their style and how urgent their requirement is, this may be a completely inappropriate conversation topic for two reasons; it positions business as the only important thing in this person's life (and, by inference, yours too) and secondly, it can make the other person feel pressured into asking you the same question when they may not feel like they know you well enough to make a referral.

Remember that while these are the details you want to capture as a result of the conversation, the most important thing is the conversation itself. Don't sacrifice making a meaningful connection with someone for the sake of an efficient data-gathering process! Just being mindful of this effective strategy is often enough to ensure that you remember to do the right things. So, be interested, ask questions that will help you get to know them better and build the mutual desire to want to stay in touch.

When you get home or next sit down to capture your details from the event, you should have enough information to be able to follow up effectively which, as we discovered earlier, is the foundation for a great network.

Meeting existing friends at a live event is slightly different for obvious reasons. You should already have their contact details, so the focus is on developing the relationship further. Have fun, be interested in their news, ask if there is anything you can do to help. When you get back to your networking scorecard, you only need to capture clear updates and follow up with any connection requests.

Online

Online networking is different for all the reasons we looked at in Chapter 5, Tools for the job, but the principles remain the same. As my friend, and Global Twitter Marketing Specialist, Keith Keller would say: 'Give, give, give... then ask.'

You should be thinking constantly, 'What can I do or say that will benefit the people in my network?'. Sometimes that may be humour, sometimes it might be a message to a specific individual and sometimes it will be something that has inspired you that you'd like to share, but it should always be done with an external focus. Anything else is pure marketing and you will find plenty of great books that can help you with that. We're talking about building relationships online and therefore, when measuring your effectiveness, the metrics need to give a sense of how well you are maintaining the relationships with the people who are most important to you. When I was writing *Mastering Time*, I referenced a phrase that was popularized at the end of the twentieth century – 'quality time'. In the book I highlighted the fact that when it came to children, quantity always outweighed quality when it came to the relationship with their parents. The same is true with the important people in your network: how much time do you spend with them (either physically or virtually)? Keeping in touch is not a chore, it's what you do when you are genuinely interested in other people. You want to know how they are, what's going on in their lives right now and when you are likely to meet up again to share some of your most precious resource, your time. Now, not everyone in your network will share this perspective, especially if they enjoy their own company most, but that is not your concern. If they are important to you, find ways of demonstrating that.

Breaking this down in more specific terms for your online networking strategy, you may find it helpful to categorize your network into groups so that you can communicate effectively and maintain good relationships and not forget anyone that is important to you.

Let's start with your 'close' relationships: who are they? Retrieve your network map to remind yourself of the key people. You will remember that some of our business networking experts talked about 'inner circles', people that you have potentially known an age (or at least it can feel like that if they are new into your circle of close friends). They may be confidantes, advisers, family, old friends, business partners but generally, they are your first port of call when you need support. As you would expect, and most people do this automatically, we want to keep in regular contact with these people. A good measure of what is important is to ask yourself these sorts of questions:

- How would I feel if someone in this group was in trouble and I wasn't aware, and therefore unable to help?
- How much richer/more fun is my life from spending time with this person?
- Who could I depend upon if I was in trouble?

Once you know who is in this group (and most people do instinctively), then, if you are connected online, keep in touch. Social media sites like

Facebook and Google+ make it easy to keep up with the news from these people, interact with them and share stuff (technical term). In many ways, social media is helping to overcome the problems created by social mobility. For example, my father was the thirteenth child in his family and, of the eight that lived beyond infancy, all of them lived in the same town for much of their adult lives. However, just in my personal family, my brothers and I all live more than two hours away from where my mum lives and about five hours away from each other. This was not planned, but has become a fact of our lives. Now, we keep in touch via Facebook, Skype, Google+ and Pinterest and, if we're feeling particularly extravagant, we pay for the odd phone call too! Some of my closest friends are also at the other end of the UK, but again, online works wonderfully.

The second specific group I want to look at are the ones we classified as being 'on the radar'. These are people that either they or I have implied that it would be useful to keep in touch with each other because there may be some mutual benefit around the corner. Remember, this is not about being a false friend that is only keeping in touch because you want something from the other; it is about becoming more familiar with the person and what they do because you may be able to help them. This is a group that online networking really supports well. Through sites like LinkedIn, you can find out a lot about someone and if you follow them on Twitter or connect with them on Facebook and Google+ you get a very rounded view of them and their real interests, providing you with many more points of potential connection. Online marketers will often cite this information as priceless in identifying your ideal customers and clients because the technology allows you to interact directly and build a relationship with almost anyone. What we're talking about here though, is ease of access. Formerly, it would have taken two people a long time to get to know each other through exclusively face-to-face meetings, and, potentially, the time investment would have been too great. Now, you can move the relationship on quicker and get to know and even like a person through digital media. Trust still takes longer and is greatly enhanced by face-to-face meetings but to have achieved the first two aspects of a great relationship relatively effortlessly is a major benefit of online networking.

Next, let's take a look inside an organization or, more specifically, a project team. I have seen project teams totally overlook the benefits of keeping in touch with their major stakeholders throughout the course of a project and thereby threaten the achievement of their objectives. Big corporate projects, or dispersed teams face the same challenge – keeping everyone informed and motivated to deliver, when getting together for one-to-one or group meetings is just infeasible on a regular basis. The temptation is to wait until just prior to the next meeting before you communicate progress or highlight problems, and this is totally counter-productive. Stakeholders and teams need to be kept informed, so having a 'networking strategy' or relationship development plan in place makes a lot of sense. Identify everyone you need to keep in touch with and then determine the best way to keep them up to date and empowered to help. If you have the luxury of having several people at your disposal, think about matching them up to one or two of the key players each as you define the following:

💬 How do they like to communicate?

💬 How frequently do we need to keep in touch for maximum awareness and sense of ownership?

💬 How can we ensure our message stands out?

💬 What else do we know about them as human beings?

This last question of course tracks back to the point we made earlier about treating everyone in your network as a person first and foremost. Even in a work context, people will still respond to you better if they sense you are genuinely interested in the things that keep them awake at night. That may be work or it could be something more personal, but listen for the clues and they will be there.

Primarily, the online nature of these relationships has traditionally been e-mail, but increasingly, this is becoming the phone, video conferences or online groups and forums set up for the purpose of the project. Ultimately, it doesn't matter how you communicate with these people as long as you can meet their expectations. Your measures will be subjective initially as you try to assess their level of commitment to the project, but over time you will be able to upgrade these with anecdotal evidence of their support or advocacy.

Finally, there is everyone else that knows you! Just how do you measure your effectiveness with the sheer volumes of people that are available to you to interact with online? Well, that depends on your networking approach and the size of your network. We talked in Chapter 2, How big should my network be?, about the different approaches to networking online, from closed to completely open and all of the hybrids in between. If you are an open networker and therefore likely to connect with anyone who requests a connection, then you might assume that being effective is merely about checking just how many people you are connected to; it's 'just a numbers game' right? Not necessarily – the key is to know *why* you are an open networker and then you can still work strategically as you grow your network. Thomas Power is the Number 1 most connected person on LinkedIn and has been for over nine years (41,820 as of August 2013), so I thought I would ask him what he is aiming to do with his extremely open networking strategy and this is what he said:

" To me networking is about Connecting people. The more you connect people the more connections you receive back. I ask people three main questions:

1 What's their expertise, and can they define it in one word?
2 What's the biggest project they're working on right now?
3 Who can I put them in touch with that can help them with that project?

Most people, when they go networking, are seeking contacts, information and deals; so, what you want to get good at, is being able to match the right contacts, with the right content in the right context. Effectively, making the right connections and following through.

Thomas Power, former Chairman of ground-breaking social business online network, Ecadamy, no.1 most connected person on LinkedIn and co-founder of Scredible Leaders

So, even the most open networker in the world advocates listening as the number one skill and measures his effectiveness by what he is able to do for the connections he makes.

At the other end of the scale are the closed networkers and, if this is the approach you choose to adopt, then you should measure your effectiveness by looking at how the relationships you have, grow and develop. One of the features of a closed network, like private members clubs, is the power of exclusivity and the general acceptance that every member has been vouched for and is therefore already 'trusted'. Consequently, the possibility of creating deals will be enhanced if the right opportunities surface. The downside of course is that, as referrals expert, Andy Lopata says, to get to the most fruitful business relationships, you may have to 'work through your network' rather than expecting deals to come from within it. Nevertheless, maintaining a sense of control of the data and the changes within your network is obviously easier if it is focused on a smaller group of individuals, so your only task is to keep up with what your network is doing and remembering what they are looking for at any point in time.

Most of our experts sit somewhere in the middle of these two approaches and have selective or hybrid networks. They may be open to approaches from individuals, but they keep in mind qualifying criteria, especially the question: 'Why do you want to connect with me online?' This group also tend to reject auto connections of the sort made popular by the LinkedIn connection request template, unless the individual looks like they might have a good reason to want to connect anyway. Depending on the nature of your current business, you may wish to capture data on where your network is going both geographically and by industry.

However you choose to build your network, the emphasis should still be on cultivating the relationships and keeping notes is a great way of helping yourself, and your network, unless, of course, you are blessed with the almost photographic recall of Thomas Power.

Show me the money

Don't count your conversations but make your conversations count.
Rob Brown, best-selling author of How to Build
Your Reputation *and Head of the*
Global Networking Council

For some reading this chapter, there will be an impatience to know when the money is going to come in as a result of all this relationship building, and while I have deliberately steered you away from thinking about the money as you build your networks, there is one measure that is worth tracking regarding Return on Investment. As you get started on your project or your business, keep a track of your expenditure in all areas of sales, marketing and promotion. Networking is just one component of a marketing strategy; it sits alongside advertising, promotions, conferences, exhibitions, sponsorship, cold calling, newsletters, structured sales processes, mail and speaking as a mechanism for generating awareness and trust to lead prospects to what you have to offer. So, by all means, measure the overall results from building relationships against these other activities to assess its validity as a marketing option. When seen in this light, networking can be extremely cost effective. Every now and again, I sit and determine where my work has come from and I am always amazed at just how much has come through my networks in some form or other. In fact, after the first six months of setting up my business, I have spent almost nothing on marketing. Virtually every piece of work I have won or been involved in has come through my networks, whether that be with local small business owners, individual mentoring clients or major corporates.

The scorecard in action

As a pragmatic person, I am always looking to see how effective things are and constantly measure. The networking scorecard is effectively the gift that just keeps on giving. You immediately set yourself apart in your networks as someone who demonstrably cares about the people you meet and are able to add value in a number of tangible ways. This can only be good for you and, if you work for someone else, their business too. Overleaf is a brief case study to illustrate the impact that the scorecard has made for just one of my clients.

CASE STUDY

A couple of years ago I was asked to help the corporate sales team of a leading high street mobile phone company. Their challenge was how to take full advantage of the multiple networking events available to the teams around the UK. Historically, the team members had viewed the events as little more than a good excuse to grab a few drinks after work and hand out a few business cards. Also, typically, as a major 'brand' they were often asked to supply prizes for the raffle or provide funds to sponsor all, or part, of the events. Unsurprisingly, therefore, managers were starting to question the expenditure on such events and the efficacy of local networking as an effective addition to their marketing strategy.

After spending some time with a selection of the national team going through the five-step plan and the networking scorecard, it was time to let them loose on a few events! Initially, the results were slow as the team focused on building relationships from scratch, but they stayed focused on the scorecard, recording and following up on every conversation. Predictably, the reputation of the individuals in the team as valued members of the various networks began to improve. The key in this case was the sharing of data from the scorecards within the team; as each person returned from an event they would record their actions and highlight connection requests in particular. Then the whole team would look at these and think if they had a connection that may be valuable. This facilitated many 'out of area' connections and spread the value of the company's outward facing network substantially.

Quicker than expected, the results began to come in as the improved reputation of the individuals within their networks elicited sales and also set the foundations of several commercial opportunities. They decided that their most significant metric on the scoreboard was 'connections made' from the requests of their networks. For them, this seemed to go hand-in-hand with referrals back from their networks. Latterly, they have aligned this strategy with a social media presence that makes it easier for their contacts to buy from them but the emphasis is still on connecting people not selling.

The Networking Scorecard

Event Name: *Retail Exhibition*

New Connections	Follow Ups Booked
Kyle Thomas *Tamzin Wright*	*Kyle Thomas*

Connection Requests	Connections Made
Kyle – Needs a Digital Designer	*Kyle and Ben Peters (LinkedIn)*

Referrals Received	Network Updates
None	*Chris Jenkins, promoted.* *Regional Director*

Expenses	Time
£60 train	*8 hours*

Key points

> *Even though you are on the right track – you will get run over if you just sit there.*
>
> Will Rogers, vaudeville performer, humorist,
> social commentator and motion picture actor

The networking scorecard keeps the most important activities and information you need to grow your network, right in front of you and transforms you into a professional relationship builder!

Coming up next, how to add a pinch of professionalism to every aspect of your networking.

The complete professional networker

A professional is someone who can do his best work when he doesn't feel like it.

Alistair Cooke, British/American journalist,
television personality and broadcaster

Throughout this book, I have aimed to break down the concept of networking into easily achieved steps and simple processes, so that you can make swift progress. To maintain momentum and build the networks you would like in your life, it is critical to implement a relatively organized approach. This ensures that the right way of doing things becomes habitual rather than a chore. Remember how we discovered that one of the most valued attributes of a networker was their overall reliability? Do they follow up? Do they make the introductions they promised? The reason is because we rely on our networks for our very existence, and the more assurance you can provide to the individuals in your networks that you will do what you say you will do, the faster your networks will grow.

In this chapter, we will review the whole networking process, highlighting a few last tips from our experts but, more importantly, seeing how you can integrate all of your activity so that you are constantly building your networks – effectively and effortlessly.

Face-to-face

The five steps

Whether it is a formal networking event, an industry conference, a work meeting or a party, it is always a good idea to keep the five steps in mind:

1 Plan – Who will be there? Who would you like to meet and why? Who might you be able to help? What will you wear? What are the timings? Where is it? Remember, some websites, like Business Scene, allow you to see who is attending, but when that isn't the case, it doesn't hurt to ask the organizer directly.

2 Meet – How can you stand out? Do you have any instantly recognizable features you could accentuate? Are you able to help the event organizer in any way, ensuring you meet many people without even trying? One person I know always has a mini questionnaire or a survey question or two to break the ice and meet people – works a treat!

3 Connect – Give the present of your presence. What connections can you make? What's the best thing you can do to help right now? What interesting things have you read recently? How can you adapt to their style of communication? Have you captured the follow-up actions?

4 Enlist – Have you spent some time developing your 'enlisting words'? Here's the format that has stood the test of time and was recommended by several of our experts: 'I specialize in... I work with... helping them to... For example,...' Just fill in the blanks.

Try it out on a few people. Is it memorable? Do you have an obvious client for referrals? Remember, enlisting is secondary, the relationship is your focus. When will you next interact with your new connections?

5 Follow up – How soon can you make promised introductions? Have you linked via all social media channels? When are you due to meet up for a one-to-one and get to know each other better? This is the step that separates the pros from the amateurs!

> *I'm a big believer in professionalism, doing what you say and saying what you do and following through! It's important for me to follow through whenever I can make a difference. That's my reputation. That's my character and that's my mindset.*
>
> Damon Lawrenson, award-winning interim Financial
> Director and prolific network builder

The power of attention

> *Give whatever you are doing and whoever you are with the gift of your attention.*
>
> Jim Rohn, motivational speaker

Networking is all about relationships, so when you meet someone that you would like to build a relationship with, doesn't it make sense to give them your attention? Life is full of distractions and opportunities to do *anything but* give others your attention. The text message, the phone call and the notification from Facebook are all designed to grab your attention, but at what cost? Almost certainly, the person with whom you are talking will excuse one interruption, especially if it is accompanied with a short apologetic explanation; but more than one and they will feel, quite rightly, that their conversation is a very low priority for you. I know this is not the correct use of the term, but this is really 'disruptive technology'. The impact is dramatic too. I've seen people leave meetings and end conversations when the person they were talking to allowed themselves to be continually interrupted.

Many people feel that their lives are one perpetual to-do list, rushing from one task to the next and never feeling like they have time for themselves.

So, when you meet them, if you can pay them some attention and remind them that they are important, you will be paying them the biggest compliment and establishing yourself as someone they want to have in their life.

All of the individuals I have interviewed for this book or have seen in action are, as you would expect, excellent at giving their undivided attention when they are with you. You really feel like you are the most important person in the room. They are not looking around for the next person to talk to and they're not glancing at their watch or their phone. Instead, they are actively listening to what you have to say and visibly enjoying the conversation.

The bridge

The gap between a first meeting and a second interaction is an important one to manage. Take control – not everyone is a professional like you! Many people come away from a networking event or other meetings and forget to follow up. You want to strike while the iron is hot and move quickly to secure a second meeting, or at least a conversation, if there is a definite opportunity for either of you. What you are doing is building the bridge between the meeting and the ongoing networking relationship. If the gap between you is not bridged you have the potential to waste the opportunity with your new connection that you cultivated when you first met. Despite the fact that this is all I wanted to say, I thought it important enough to warrant its own heading. In effect, I'm talking about following up, but the concept of building something really helps me to focus on this activity whereas following up can sound and feel a bit passive or routine at best.

Online success

Once you have created the bridge between your offline and online activities, success comes down to your ability to maintain your networks and further develop the relationships you have built. To do that, you need to recognize the fluid nature of your relationships. As the poem says:

People come into your life for a reason, a season or a lifetime.
When you figure out which one it is,
you will know what to do for each person.

Unknown

Online networking makes it easier to divide people into groups with which you can thrive as well as provide support. Not seeing your networks as one big group will help you to develop better relationships with everyone. You will want to keep in regular contact with your close contacts, but more distant acquaintances would probably view regular contact as a nuisance. Developing a rough contact strategy will help enormously, so let's get started.

Contacts for a reason

Sometimes we are working on a project at work or in life and the people we are working with need to be kept close to ensure that everyone is informed or feels able to contribute fully. In project management terms, these people are called stakeholders, which is a great label because it is basically everyone who has a stake in what is being done. Sharing information, resources, contacts and updates is essential and so these groups should always be prioritized in your networking strategy. If the project is significant, there will be many stakeholders, so map them out and consider putting them into a spreadsheet or a CMS (contact management system) application to help you decide how often you would like to keep in touch, what are the key messages or decisions you will want to share and a running log of when you last interacted with them to ensure they don't fall off the radar for a few weeks!

Talking of radars, I always have a small list of people who are 'on my radar' and by that I mean, either I anticipate I may be able to help them soon or vice versa. For example, I recently met a young man who is starting a new business, manufacturing and selling frozen yoghurt. While this is an established market in the United States, it is a relatively scarce product in the United Kingdom – and I love it! As soon as he is ready, I have a couple of people lined up to introduce to him. That will definitely be a win–win, when I can buy his products in my local supermarkets. Meanwhile, I keep a watching brief on his profile and I am constantly on the lookout for useful articles to send links.

Contacts for a season

When we connect with another individual, we seldom have any idea how significant that connection will be. Will they be someone who merely posts the odd amusing or interesting article? Will they become a trusted adviser (even if they don't know it)? Will they become involved in a significant joint project? Will they become great friends? Who knows? However, the law of averages would suggest that most relationships are more seasonal than lifelong, so with this in mind, we need a relationship maintenance strategy that doesn't feel like it's a chore and, instead, is meaningful (from everyone's perspective).

Generally, our experts suggest a strategy which imitates what you do offline – focus on the relationship and be supportive when you can. What this means in terms of online activity is sharing broadly any items that grab your attention and more specifically when you can think of an individual or a group that would benefit from something that you see, or an introduction to someone that you meet. Don't worry about the content of what you share, if it interests you, then that is a valid enough reason to post it online. Your close friends will give you any feedback required if your content is not presenting you in the best light. Just remember that the networking purpose of your presence online is to support your network – sometimes that can be with a few wise words and sometimes that can come from just being yourself!

Contacts for a lifetime

This group may include family, close friends and other people that developed from 'seasonal friends' into 'lifetime friends' and the great news is that this is what some of the more social networks were designed to support. Think about the things that populate the timeline on the world's biggest online network, Facebook – photos, video links, jokes, tags, news and gossip. These are, for many people, the social ties that bind them together for a lifetime. The ability to keep in touch at the touch of a button (or screen) is reinforcing relationships that logistically would have otherwise dissipated. It keeps friends in your network closer. I have many great friends that live several hours away from me and, even if we only saw each other once a year, we would still pick up where we left off last time, with no detrimental impact on our relationship. What Facebook does is enhance the feeling of connection when we are apart. If I can see family photos, holiday updates or career changes in front of my eyes and make a comment, then, emotionally, I am with them. The difference between this and phone calls is that a phone call is usually timed according to availability, whereas updates are made in a timely fashion and available to read as soon as the reader is online. However, be careful not to over-exaggerate the ability of online networking – it is, at best, only a supplement to offline conversations and meetings. Sometimes, a warm smile, a big hug or a congratulatory slap on the back are the only things that will hit the spot in a close relationship.

New contacts

First, having read all about the various approaches that our experts take to build their networks, you need to decide what strategy you are going to deploy online. Will you adopt an open or a closed approach, or something in between?

The closed online networker seeks out known and established connections and only joins online groups that are related to their offline equivalent. They tend to ignore connection requests from anyone that they do not already know, unless they are recommended by an existing trusted contact. As a result, their online network is a digital version of their existing relationships. Obviously, this is an attractive approach as it comes with an established degree of comfort, minimal decision making and maximum efficiency. As discussed earlier, the key problem is one of missing out on opportunities that may arise outside of a closed network.

The open networker online accepts all connection requests and values the so-called law of weak connections which highlights the remote origin of most opportunities within any given network. The challenge comes in managing your time and focus with an extensive open network, which is why one of the greatest exponents of open networking, Thomas Power, stresses the need for a new mindset if you are truly going to embrace an open strategy – away from controlling to accepting the randomness associated with free connecting.

I don't use any judgment around the data sets I receive. I can receive any volume of data sets, in any angle, in any context; or any subject, in any location, at any time. Then I focus on making that connection.

So my technique is open, random and supportive. It's non-judgmental and I'm only looking for an outcome for the other person.
Thomas Power, former Chairman of ground-breaking social business online network, Ecademy, no. 1 most connected person on LinkedIn and co-founder of Scredible Leaders

The hybrid approaches between these extremes combine the focus of closed networking with the bigger opportunity in an open approach. Many of our experts operate a 'selective' approach which has room for connections with unknown people, but only if some qualifying criteria are met. Many of them, for example, automatically reject the auto connect requests from LinkedIn, but this has its own flaws because many LinkedIn mobile apps do not allow the individual to send a note with their connection request, so you have to be careful how you apply your strategy. Others enter into a small dialogue to understand why the individual wishes to connect, which overcomes this particular issue.

Personally, my hybrid approach is on the verge of being completely open. As I said earlier, I am open to connection requests without question on LinkedIn because I believe that if a restaurant owner in the United States, or a dentist in India, wants to connect with me, then I have the potential to make two new friends and both of us have the opportunity to meet people in our networks that the other may have a good enough relationship with to make a meaningful referral. You really just never know. Where I apply a slightly closed approach is on the more social networks such as Facebook. I only share certain family photos with close connections and I wouldn't necessarily accept every connection request either, for two principal reasons: (1) Facebook only allows 5,000 personal connections and if you exceed this limit you have just acquired another job of managing connections in and out of your network; (2) I don't think my 'social only' status updates add value to anyone outside of my existing networks. My early experiments of connecting to unknown individuals didn't result in any meaningful conversations (either way) so I am content to interact with new people through other online networks such as LinkedIn, Twitter and Google+. The challenge is to come up with a strategy that allows you to connect to people without sacrificing your ability to build great relationships with your closest connections.

Here's a tongue-in-cheek insight of how one of the most prolific users of all social media deals with the thorny problem of the Facebook friend limit:

> *I am in the process of going through 600 friend requests here on Facebook. Here's why I didn't follow or friend you: 1. You don't write in English. 2. You don't put your job title on Facebook (almost always that's a good indicator of someone who doesn't put good content into Facebook). 3. You only have baby photos on your wall. That's cool for your family, but I'm looking for something more. 4. You have no friends in common with me. Listen, I have 5,000 friends and they are well curated from across the tech industry. If you can't make friends with a few of those people then I've found that to be a good marker that you really aren't into tech. 5. You have cat photos on your wall. 6. You friended me then you ran out of friend spaces (Facebook limits us both to 5,000*

total friends). 7. You only have food and wine posts on your wall. 8. You have fewer than 10 posts total. 9. You have your privacy turned up so high I can't see anything about you (I hate that, make yourself easier to check out if you're gonna friend me). 10. No meat. I'm not talking about Turkey meat. I'm talking about posts that actually say something deep about who you are, what you are passionate about, and what you care about. If all you got is selfies I probably won't be friending you. Even then I can't friend everyone so it's a bit of a lottery after that. Looking for people who bring me great content. Still have 300 requests to go. Yes, if I've met you face-to-face I'm more likely to friend you. Extra points if you got me a great whiskey... How do you decide whether to friend someone? One other tip? Make it possible for me to follow you. I'm far more liberal with those than the friend thing.

Robert Scoble, best known for his blog, Scobleizer,
which came to prominence during his tenure as a
technology evangelist at Microsoft

Whichever approach you choose, here's a helpful list of some online activities that a number of our experts and I do to develop powerful networks that can support us in all of our endeavours:

- Put aside small pockets of time to engage your networks – many experts talked of only two or three 30-minute slots per week.

- Prioritize your time to focus initially on both close and project-based relationships.

- Utilize web tools such as Hootsuite's Hootlet and Share buttons to capture information and links *while you are surfing* for immediate distribution to your network contacts.

- Dip into LinkedIn groups to answer questions arising from your network or to share with your network to source some answers.

- Ask questions when you need support – it is not a sign of weakness; in fact, it provides an obvious cue to someone to continue to build their relationship with you.

- Review your 'On the Radar' list and send a note of encouragement or a link to something useful for them.

- Make introductions where you can, or when requested. (Note: many people raised the point of only wanting to make good introductions as their reason for not accepting people that they didn't know into their networks, but I have a different view. I am happy to introduce someone that I do not know well in my network and I will always accompany the introduction with an explanation of my lack of personal insight and their need to verify and validate any credentials presented by the individual concerned.)

- Share useful information with your network: interesting articles, new policies or laws, updates within your network, videos or testimonials that highlight the expertise of your networks.

- Write and share information related to your own business, job or industry to help your network and to promote your own value and expertise.

Of course, the principles behind all of these items are also applicable offline – the key is to be consistent.

If you manage to do this, you will not find your extensive network overwhelming, in fact you will start to appreciate just how much more information and real contacts are at your fingertips when trying to solve problems or gather information.

How not to network

 Be a Resource, not a Salesperson.

Keith Keller, Global Twitter Marketing Specialist

It is very easy to get it all wrong. We have heard how the experts agree that their pet hate are people who thrust business cards into their hands before they have established rapport but this list of other common errors may also provide you with some insight:

Only talk about your work – don't waste your time chatting about things that the other person may find interesting (like themselves) as this will only lead to you having to talk to them longer or, even worse, getting to know them! Even at an industry conference or a work seminar, only talking about work can make it difficult for people to connect with you on an emotional level. Obviously, within a professional context, you need to be careful not to let the conversation veer into areas best preserved for the pub or wine bar, but discussions that involve elements of self-disclosure around family or personal interests can be a source of additional connection between you and your network contacts. When it's time for business, talk business, but don't let that be the only point of connection, all the time.

Be a closed person – there's no point in letting other people know your true motives; just get in, extract everything you need with minimum fuss and get out again. Like a networking ninja, hopefully, no-one will have even noticed you were there. Leading on from only talking about work, if you are the sort of person who likes to play your cards close to your chest, then you may need to reassess how you go about networking. Being closed is recognizable by others as not sharing why you are interested in a particular topic or only asking questions and never leaving space for others to ask questions of you. This does not necessarily become apparent to others immediately, but suddenly, someone will ask them a question about you and they will be surprised at how little they know or, more frequently, they will be left feeling 'uneasy' about you. I had someone like this in my network recently. He was very happy to meet new people and share an interesting message but he shared nothing of himself or what personally motivated him and individual after individual shared with me and others a number of familiar phrases concerning their feelings about him; 'there's something about him that makes me feel uneasy,' and 'I just couldn't put my finger on it but something isn't right.' The quickest way to build trust is through transparency and a genuine congruency between what you say and how you feel about what you say.

Be selfish – look at who is in a network and think only of how you can help yourself to their knowledge and resources, while keeping all of yours firmly in place. The most successful networks are ones in which all of the networkers seek to give, support and help others with no thought of reciprocity. The least successful networkers are those that seek only to gain from their networks; this behaviour is representative of a limited view of the world's resources, scarcity thinking. It is most evident in the way people share their networks. Selfish networkers seek to keep their networks all to themselves and do not share their connections for fear that they will lose some sort of advantage. The reality is completely opposite to this – by connecting people in your networks, you are demonstrating their value, reinforcing your desire to help them and, indirectly, generating a halo for yourself.

Ignore people – next time you are at an event or online, make sure you ignore the people that are seeking to connect or reconnect with you. After all, they will only eat up your time and soak up all of your energy and you're a busy person! Of course, you may find that you are not as busy as you would like if you continue to ignore people as it will certainly damage those relationships and, over time, your credibility too.

Focus on the hospitality – the great thing about all of these networking opportunities is the abundance of food and drink that is available, especially at work events. Help yourself to as much as possible, after all, just think of how eloquent and liberated you will feel to really speak your mind! Every company has its stories of individuals that 'drank too much at the office party' and made a CLM (Career Limiting Move). Only you will know your capacity to drink without approaching your limits, adhere to them wisely and, if being out late is something you enjoy, supplement your alcohol with water to remain coherent and mindful. I know many of our experts who really enjoy a drink but refuse to imbibe until the formal networking is over and then always keep things to a manageable level unless they are among really close friends.

Develop an inner circle

The Master Mind may be defined as… Coordination of knowledge and effort, in a spirit of harmony, between two or more people, for the attainment of a definite purpose.

Napoleon Hill, from Think and Grow Rich

One of the most powerful networks you can create over time is an inner circle. Essentially, this is a small group of close connections with whom you are able to share your personal and professional challenges, openly. In return for your openness and your support for them, this group provide you with any number of benefits, including:

- sounding board for approaching a problem;
- test group for new ideas;
- strategic insights;
- forum for letting off steam;
- personal guidance;
- confidential advice; and
- introductions and qualified referrals.

The mastermind principle that was most famously discussed in Napoleon Hill's *Think and Grow Rich* reveals the real power of small groups of mutually supportive individuals. They say that your wealth can usually be calculated by averaging that of your five closest friends, so once one individual starts to move forward in a group, the whole group begins to advance, together, probably by association and shared new knowledge. Most of our experts shared stories of how their personal inner circle had helped them at critical points in their development or in life in general. These are not always groups set up for the purpose of helping each other; quite often, inner circles are made up of individuals that you encounter in different areas of your life; maybe a parent, a sibling, an old friend, a close colleague, a college room-mate or a group of industry peers. The key is that you have a few people you can rely on when you are facing a challenge.

As your career develops, it becomes more and more important to nurture your relationships with a group you can trust completely, a group with integrity and your interests at heart. Trust and integrity are critical and the two characteristics that our experts stressed above all others when it comes to putting your inner circle together. Who can you trust implicitly and who has the integrity to advise you selflessly with no thought of personal gain?

 The problem with entrepreneurs is that we have new ideas all the time... that doesn't mean they are good! It certainly doesn't mean they

should always be acted upon. My network has acted like a review board for my ideas, only letting the best ones through and then helping develop those like an incubator.

Warren Cass, founder and CEO of Business Scene Membership Ltd

Life without an inner circle

I produced the diagram opposite to help a homeless charity explain the real causes of homelessness for a campaign they were running to help overcome widely-held assumptions about street dwellers, such as they are there by choice or through criminal activity. In fact, most of the individuals I met that had found themselves homeless, were highly ethical citizens who had fallen on extremely bad luck. Their bad luck was compounded by a breakdown in their personal support networks. As the figure illustrates, they did not have a foundation of the people that many of us are fortunate enough to be able to rely on, such as parents and siblings. Consequently, there was no-one around when their financial or emotional accounts were empty. If we were to look at your networks from a Maslov 'hierarchy of needs' perspective, we are talking here about the very basic level, your security. Your ability to branch out, make a living and expand your life can only really gain momentum once you have this fundamental network firmly established.

The strategic networker

The final tool in the effective networker's kit is the ability to think and act strategically. This all starts by answering the question, 'Why are you networking?' We've provided you with dozens of reasons why you should network in this book, but you need to decide what your key motivators are. Is it to get ahead at work? Is it to expand your business options? Is it to improve your social life or is it just to smooth your path through life? Whatever your reason, it will serve you better if you decide what it is and then determine how you will make it happen – strategically.

As we go through life, different networks will play an important role at different times. The strategically minded networker simply decides which ones to tap into when faced with a specific challenge. For example, rather than sending out a generic message to everyone when looking for a new supplier, the strategic networker will identify their top targets and then

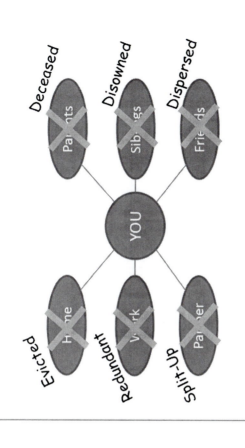

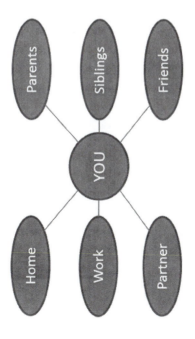

CASE STUDY

Heidi Smith runs a small, and growing, international company that is in a well-defined niche – Russian Paralegals! However, far from being an easy business to grow, Heidi faces a number of challenges that include keeping a geographically dispersed team motivated and maintaining a steady flow of customers and new business in the pipeline. One of the most interesting challenges Heidi shared with me was the need to manage her time carefully when it came to the sheer number of networking events available to her. In sharing her thinking, Heidi reveals some of the key elements of the strategic networker:

As with everything I do within my business, my networking strategy is based on a process that I've thought through and I've planned. It is integrated with my marketing plan and my marketing strategy and it's based around contacting the people who can most likely refer business to me in the future. Everybody in my network is categorized according to the type of contact that they are and then I have a process around my networking that allows me to stay in touch with the right people at a period of time that I think they would be interested to hear from me, but not so frequently that they're going to get fed up with me getting in contact with them. It's based on a strategy that I think allows me to provide practical and useful help to people in my network so that I'm offering things to them, not always taking things from them. And my approach is ... my aim, rather, is to try and be at the top of people's mind at the right point, so that when they do have a need for our services, I'm the first person that comes to mind or my business is the first business that comes to mind for exactly the right sort of services that we're offering.

Heidi Smith, founder and Director of www.russianparalegals.com

determine how they are going to get close to them. It's this type of thinking that is behind the notions of 'degrees of separation'. How many levels of connection are there between you and your target person? If you are an open networker it will probably be less than for a closed networker or, more importantly, the more effort you have invested in building relationships and developing an inner circle, the quicker your route through to the valuable connections you seek.

Sometimes, however, it is not obvious who you need to contact. If this is the case, the most useful strategy is to spread your net widely, brushing against as wide a group as possible. Remember that your potential referrers come in all shapes and sizes, with different preferences in terms of both style of network and timing. In fact this last point is really important and simple to plan into your networking schedule. The self-confessed 'least strategic networker' that I interviewed utilizes this fact extremely well:

> I network at different times of the day because you meet different people. I like to try a variation of breakfast, lunch and evening events, because as well as meeting a variety of people, you meet people in different frames of mind.
>
> Debbie Tarrier, former host of South Coast Connections
> and voice-over artist and presenter

Maximized effectiveness

I always tell my clients when we're working through the mastering time strategies that the more you try to do yourself the longer success will take because you'll always run out of hours in the day to get things done. Your networks are a source of immense capacity and, typically, a very willing partner in moving you forward.

This is particularly true for service providers where the value of a referral outweighs a cold contact almost exponentially. Strategic relationships are critical if you want to get the word out about what you are doing and bring a surge of referrals into your business.

Strategic relationships include joint ventures (like the one between Simon Ellinas and me on this book), associations (like the many informal groups that emerge from industry networks), collaborations (often between complementary service providers) and referral partnerships (like the ones developed through closed networks). The key is to think win–win as we discussed earlier. Who may share your objectives and be interested in pairing up to achieve them? How might referring you be of value to them? Are your services appropriate for their connections in terms of content and perceived value? How will clients gain from your collaboration?

This is not necessarily a complex process, in fact many of the best strategic relationships are already within your networks, you just haven't had the appropriate conversation with them yet. You need to arrange a face-to-face meeting and let them know what you are seeking to achieve. With just a handful of strategic relationships you can quickly and dramatically expand your access to your target market. They can help you get in the door, face-to-face, with key decision makers much more easily, and even better, these prospects will be more receptive to meeting with you as a warm referral from an already trusted connection.

The bottom line is strategic relationships are very powerful and they can also be very easy to build, easier than you think, when you have put the work in and built the right foundations.

Key points

 Success is almost totally dependent upon drive and persistence. The extra energy required to make another effort or try another approach is the secret of winning
                    Denis Waitley, author and high performance lecturer

- Much of what it takes to do anything professionally is a desire to accept setbacks with the mindset that says 'Is there a better way of doing this and, if not, what can I learn from this experience?'

- You now have all you need to network effectively; if you've done the job properly, you can mobilize it at any time!

Mobilizing your network

> *Untapped potential is the difference between where a person is now and where he or she can be.*
>
> *Bo Bennett, author, researcher, entrepreneur*

Apparently, the average computer software user utilizes less than 10 per cent of the available functionality. Depending on your learning style, it is very likely that you've never read a manual or a user guide in your life, preferring instead to play with the application until you stumble upon the requisite function. This is why software developers invented 'Help' that pops up or is available on demand rather than in advance – they know how good we are at leaving untapped the wealth of useful information. Unfortunately, the same is true of the way many people utilize their networks – even though the opportunities that lie within are almost limitless! Ask yourself: when was the last time you put a request out to your network? Who would you go to first if you had a thorny business problem? If you wanted to find out what good looked like in your industry, where would you start?

The answers are all out there, waiting for you to ask the right questions. Your network can transform your effectiveness in so many ways and, in this chapter, we are going to explore how you can tap into that power to generate the referrals you need to move you closer towards your goals.

Finally, we'll take a look at what the experts think is going to happen in the field of networking over the next 10 years and I'll share some thoughts of my own too.

Getting started

As we discussed in Chapter 2, 'How big should my network be?', your networks expand outward from you, but not necessarily uniformly or in a focused way. Often new people enter your networks in big groups as you enter new ventures or join a new organization. In such circumstances, it can be difficult to know where to focus your attention, but the key is to stay 'in the moment' and just work on each relationship as you go. Equally, if your network is growing slowly, it can be easy to let the days and weeks slip by without moving into action to follow up effectively and arrange that all-important meeting. Stay consistent and introduce routines if you are struggling. Many of our experts talked of daily and weekly activities to maintain and build their networks. Once a routine has become a habit, you can let your subconscious take over and guide you through your many meetings, summits and conferences, constantly adding to your professional network – effortlessly. However you get started, keep these words in mind:

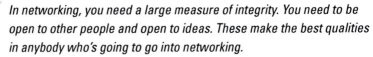

> In networking, you need a large measure of integrity. You need to be open to other people and open to ideas. These make the best qualities in anybody who's going to go into networking.
>
> *Mike Turner, Managing Director of Music Bus*

In Chapter 4, 'How to work the room', we looked at different ways that you can be both memorable and effective in your face-to-face networking, but I'd like to address the questions that people ask all the time about the process of meeting people, from saying 'hello' through to leaving a conversation elegantly. So here are a few thoughts to get you started:

- Do some 'queue networking' as Heather White calls it. Rather than stand there looking at your phone or the floor, turn to your neighbour and say 'hi' when you are stuck in a queue or a slow-moving line. From there, you could proceed to...

- The 'how' questions: How are you? How did you travel here today? How are you finding the show/conference/seminar/party so far?

- The 'what' questions: What do you do? What are you doing next? What's happening next? What do you think about (something that has just happened)? What are you hoping to get out of today/this event?

- These should keep you going long enough to break the ice, then you can ask some good questions to see if you can help them in any way, such as: 'What's keeping you awake at night?' 'What's the biggest thing you are working on at the moment?'

- Finally, we get to the process that people dread the most – moving on:

  - basic: identify someone else in the room that you would like to talk to before the end of the break/the event and ask if it would be okay to go (generally okay, but you are still leaving them on their own potentially);

  - better: welcome a third person into your conversation and then excuse yourself (although no-one is left on their own, the newly invited person may feel short-changed);

  - best: introduce your new contact to someone else you know, if you think there would be some mutual value (this is even better if you remember to give both parties an introduction to live up to).

A networking mentality

Never doubt that a small group of thoughtful, committed citizens can change the world; indeed, it's the only thing that ever has.

Margaret Mead, cultural anthropologist

I have often spoken about my inability to see 'teams' when I am working with my clients. I see individuals focused on a mutual goal, each seeking to satisfy their own needs or desires. The fact that groups of people come together to work or play does not instantaneously transform them into a team, which is why the sports teams packed full of the most expensive or talented individual players do not necessarily win all of the trophies. To even make a start on becoming a team, individuals need to be galvanized around a shared goal or higher purpose. Why am I talking about this? Well, because fundamentally, the best networkers display the best teamwork, even when they are working with just one other individual. The driving thought process when seeking support or assistance from the other people in their network is: 'How can I help them as they seek to help me?' They adopt a win–win attitude and do their best to create the circumstances in which their network associates can benefit either immediately or in the foreseeable future from helping them get what they want or need today. Of course, it is not always possible to do this and that is when your value as a trusted person in the network will become important. If you have established a reputation as someone with high integrity or you are dependable or fundamentally honest (or all three), then it is easy for your associates to support you, without thought of immediate gain. The 'win' for them may be as simple as seeing a trusted individual in their network succeed.

Regardless of your situation, you will make quick progress if you are 'open' about what you are proposing. Whether it is a referral you need, a deal you are putting together or some information that will help you overcome a significant hurdle, approach your contacts and network friends in a simple and direct fashion. Don't seek to dress it up or make it any more than it is; which is, merely, a request. Give them the opportunity to decline your request gracefully if they wish and you will find that the majority of people will be only too happy to help.

What we are getting into here is the process of referrals, an area which is richly covered by some of the greatest networkers on the planet.

Referrals

This is where all of your hard work starts to pay off, both in terms of your value to your networks and the value of your networks to you. The effort you have put into supporting your networks and gaining their trust can now be drawn upon and, if the time is right, you can ask for the help that you need. Don't try to short-cut the process; rushing to ask a new contact for referrals before you have invested in them and they have had an opportunity to grow to like and trust you, will only serve to make them feel uncomfortable at best. Better to work with your trusted advisers and close friends and colleagues to launch a mini campaign. In fact, it's not a bad idea to establish some referral exchanges with one or two individuals in your industry or in the wider business circle, so that the generation of leads becomes more of a continual process rather than an occasional chore!

Mobilizing your networks not only requires you to ask for help, it also helps you to refine what it is you need. For example, all the time an idea or a problem is stuck in your head, it will lack focus. However, as soon as you start talking about it with your networks you will face questions that will force you to think about it in more depth, increasing your certainty and making it easier to identify the resources you need to move forward. Almost always, the main 'resource' you will need is in the form of another human being – either to help you do the thing that needs to be done or to facilitate an introduction to someone who can help you do the thing that needs to be done! So how do you go about getting that referral?

Be clear and specific

The human brain craves simplicity, especially in today's world of 24/7 media and constant connectivity. We just don't seem to have the mental capacity to spend the time to pick through complexity to discover what lies behind the information or presentation before us. If the meaning behind a message is not instantaneously understood, the recipient is likely to move on and forget everything. One of the biggest favours you can do for your network is to be both clear and specific when making your requests. Before making your request, make sure you are clarifying the 5W's and 1H questions. Here's an example request from someone seeking a job opportunity:

> I am looking for a new job (What) as the current one is not stretching me enough (Why). Ideally, it would be based in Switzerland (Where), so that I can practice my skiing too. I am immediately available (When) and if you can introduce me via e-mail (How) to one or two of your Retail contacts there (Who), that would be great.

That should work a treat; or will it?

Before we jump too far ahead, let's just make sure we have the basics in place, because that unsolicited request above will return precisely zero unless you have done a few fundamentals first.

Do your research

What sets you apart in the eyes of your clients or colleagues? What makes you unique? Well, the quickest and best way to find out is to ask them. After all, they are the ones who have selected you over your competitors or promoted you to your current role. They can provide you with great insight and, importantly, in their own words, which will be very different to the ones you might use if you were asked to describe yourself.

Asking for feedback has two benefits – one that you may expect and one you may not. The first is a heightened awareness of your strengths and weaknesses which you may want to tweak and the second is a greater sense of engagement between you and the people with whom you are talking. That engagement is priceless because it leads to unexpected referrals. I have utilized a number of ways to get personal feedback in recent years from some of the closest friends in my networks; from one-to-one conversations, through to structured e-mails and even mini-surveys. Each time, I have received ideas and referrals that have enabled me to move my projects forward. In an organizational context, think of your appraisal as a key time for getting great testimonials and enlisting another powerful advocate. Think about it: how often do you get uninterrupted time to sit and have a decent professional conversation with your boss? How often do they get an opportunity to give you structured feedback and, critically, reflect on the great job you do? It may have never occurred to them in the whirlwind of day-to-day activity, that you are an individual with your own career aspirations. Prioritize getting feedback all the time, not just at appraisal time, and your referral network will grow effortlessly.

Blow your trumpet

Once armed with some fantastic feedback, you can extend your influence beyond your existing referral network and fine tune your message for the next group. The key here is to focus on the benefits of working with you, not your job title. So, if your network is telling you that they admire the clarity of your communication, don't respond to the 'What do you do for a living?'

question with, 'I'm a Tax Adviser'. Instead, try something like: 'I turn tax jargon into clear actions that my clients tell me saves them hundreds of hours a year.'

The great thing about this approach is that, if you are shy, you do not sound boastful; in fact, you can make it even more humble by adding a phrase like, 'which is what inspires me to get out of bed every morning' to the end of your introduction. What you are doing here is communicating your passion and that's what makes you memorable and inspires them to talk about you.

Seek advice, not referrals

The request I fashioned above, with its 5W's and 1H, will only generate a bundle of referrals for you if the context is right. What I mean by that is, if you just ask for it outright, either face-to-face or via e-mail, the person you are asking may have a few challenges; first is that the request has just landed without any additional information to give it texture and substance, so it may not register; second, they may have very good reasons why they cannot refer you just now (maybe they are seeking their own referrals from your target group) and finally, it is hugely assumptive to just expect a positive response. As I mentioned earlier in the book, always give your network contacts wriggle room and make it easy for them to say 'no' or, even better, don't ask them in the first place.

'Hold on', I hear you cry, 'I thought this was all about getting referrals; if we don't ask, we won't get, right?' Wrong.

By far the majority of effective referrals, and their superior cousins, recommendations, come from individuals that have had an opportunity to engage first their head and then, possibly, their heart. Essentially, this requires time. You can provide this by asking them for advice. So, you can still share the benefits your network contacts have identified and let them know that you are seeking to expand your business or increase your profile in the industry, but the question you ask is not about 'who' they can talk to on your behalf, but 'how' would they go about achieving your goal? As I said above, the solution to most business problems can be found in human beings, so their response to your question will, almost certainly, involve a recommendation to speak to someone else in their network.

Once you have done this a few times, it becomes second nature and, like most matters of courtesy, it will mark you out as a true professional and someone who others will always be happy to refer on to their connections without hesitation.

So, it turns out our 5W's and 1H request wasn't as effective as we thought it was, but don't discard it yet. It was effective, you just need to provide it at the right time – when it is requested. Right after your network contact and next best referrer has determined that there is someone in their network that may be able to help you, they will ask for more specific information and you now have a formula for providing it. Offer to do the work for them with a draft e-mail or a note for a phone conversation and they will be even more delighted to help.

Thanks and thanks again

Recently, I re-read *Endless Referrals* by Bob Burg and realized just how much his thinking has influenced mine in all of the years since I first read it in 1994. Bob is a giant in the field of referrals and generating business results through relationships and, if this is an area of particular interest to you, I would wholeheartedly recommend all of his work. One thing that Bob stresses is the importance of saying 'thank you' to the people that refer you on to their contacts. There are two reasons for this: you are letting the referrer know that their recommendation was valued and you are also informing them that the connection was actually made. The long-term bonus is that you are further developing the relationship with your referral network and increasing your chances of obtaining referrals in the future.

A moment in time

One last note about referrals and recommendations: you never know when you might need them, so be sure to 'dig your well' all the time. Networking is an activity that will serve you for a lifetime, providing you with many great experiences and opportunities, but leaving it until you need some connections is sometimes too late. Constantly nurture your network using the caring principle and it will look after you. As we saw from the example in Chapter 1, in putting this project together, I was able to draw on the expertise of a broad, knowledgeable and experienced group of individuals from across the world. Many I have known for many years, but some came from proactive referrals from within the network; from individuals who spotted a way they could help me and, indirectly, help you! South African businessman and powerboat enthusiast, Grant Harrison sums it up brilliantly:

" *I have never ever done business with anyone from the outset. My networking, I believe, is all developed through a very subtle manner of working on a continual basis over a period of time and could probably go into years before any real business has developed from it. I'm very successful at developing a very subtle business relationship.*

Grant Harrison, former Chair of the Institute of Directors for Hampshire and the Isle of Wight and also Board Director of Solent India Business Network

The future of networking

I asked all of our experts what they thought would happen in the next 10 years in the field of networking and most agreed that face-to-face would become even more prominent, despite the anticipated continued growth of online social networks. The main reason for their insistence on the sustainability of this traditional method of building relationships was the pace at which mobile technology was expanding – particularly in countries that have had less access to PCs, laptops and tablets. Used smartphones can be found all over the world and the race to develop the connecting infrastructure is well under way. While video calls are not exactly live meetings, they do offer a greater sense of connection than other digital formats and they do play a big role in personal lives, even if they have not penetrated the professional world to the extent previously anticipated.

Nevertheless, our experts did not foresee a big decline in the number of live meetings either. In fact, many thought, at a basic level, that face-to-face meetings would continue to provide the main building blocks for great relationships; whether it be following up an online connection or meeting people for the first time, most felt this to be a preferable way to operate.

Certainly, there are numerous examples of whole supply chains being sewn together on a virtual basis. Indeed, the number of people I have worked with, on a significant basis, over the past three years, that I have never met, is well into the twenties. Some of our experts run entire global businesses online and via their mobile. Many of them are called in as experts to advise multinational companies on how to develop a networked organization that can operate effectively utilizing mobile and cloud-based technology.

However, I'd like to direct you, the reader, towards an emerging opportunity that is already transforming the way we see the world. Earlier in the book, we discussed the increasing breakdown of geographically co-located families and with it, the diminishment of community for many. People are feeling isolated and alone, despite living in the most populated towns and cities in global history. This breeds fear and enhances stress levels. What Facebook, Google+, YouTube, Pinterest, LinkedIn and the plethora of other social media sites is illustrating, very clearly, is our desire to connect with others and feel connected. Part of feeling connected is to feel valued and that our lives have meaning. The ever-expanding (digital) library of books on the subject of the 'search for meaning' is both validating and codifying what it means to be human. We are social animals and where there is a vacuum of groups or community, we work very quickly to fill it.

Net weaving

About 30 years ago, Vanda North wrote an article for the SALT network which, in hindsight, perfectly describes the approach to building networks that I have sought to implement for the past 10 years. Vanda wrote of the weaving together of different educational networks on a global basis to make education better. This is not to be confused with the term 'net weaving' that has been used in recent years to simply describe the approach that all of the best networkers take (and that I have been sharing with you throughout this book) – namely, focus first on giving to your network, without thought of personal gain, and the rewards will come as the level of trust you are generating grows.

Net weaving, as described by Vanda, is focused on the exponential value in joining two or more networks and letting the individuals therein dictate where it will go. In my own experience, this was the idea behind the first 'connections' event I designed while working with Warren Cass of Business

Scene. The resultant event weaved together about nine existing networks and several corporate sponsors for one evening of shared knowledge and social connection.

The applications of this type of thinking are significant for our world. Bringing networks together can provide insights into many social problems and highlight opportunities for improvement, as this story from some of the work of the RSA illustrates:

We have done some work in a neighbourhood in Blackburn to map the social networks and start to make connections between the needs in that community and the resources in that community. For example, we found out that one of the big problems in this estate is public health. But then when you ask people what they're good at, one of the things that a lot of people say is that they're good at cooking. So there's an obvious opportunity there to say, 'Okay, what if we got all the people who enjoy cooking to work with the people whose diet isn't very good.' We're looking at social networks, looking at assets, looking at needs, and that process starts to generate new conversations. It's amazing. I firmly believe that if we were able to map networks in every community, it would on its own generate all sorts of energy and activity because people are fascinated by this stuff. The more social analysis, such as the

> *number of people who are unemployed or the number of single mothers, is just data; you share it with people, and they go, 'So what?' But when you show people a social network map and say these are the networks on your estate, people are fascinated by it, 'Oh, I see. So if I connected to that person or I'm the only person who connects to this community or that community, oh, wow!' So I think our work is brilliant and lots and lots of local authorities and others are interested in that.*
>
> *Matthew Taylor, Chief Executive of the RSA*

This is the icing on the cake of what people are doing with an enhanced knowledge of social networks. I read examples every week of groups of people that are coming together, of their own volition, to tackle problems that were previously perceived to be beyond the reach of the average person. By identifying linkages in networks, developing collaborative ventures and refusing to believe that there isn't a solution out there somewhere, we are achieving amazing things – collectively. The online tools are enabling groups to come together to address niche issues and the result is an avalanche of charitable and socially inspired activity. In the UK alone there are over 160,000 registered charities. It would appear that the desire to 'make a difference' and feel connected is gathering pace.

Key points

> *It really boils down to this: that all life is interrelated. We are all caught in an inescapable network of mutuality, tied into a single garment of destiny. Whatever affects one destiny, affects all indirectly.*
>
> *Martin Luther King*

- Referrals are the outcome of serving your network; of being resourceful, of being creative of being concerned for the well-being of others.

- We will not solve today's problems with the same level of thinking that created them. We need to continually think differently and weave our own networks together to find new solutions to the challenges we face as individuals and as co-habitants of our green planet!

Index

Also available from **Kogan Page**

ISBN: 978 0 7494 7154 5 Paperback April 2014

Order online at **www.koganpage.com**

Find out more; visit **www.koganpage.com** and
sign up for offers and regular e-newsletters.

Also available from **Kogan Page**

ISBN: 978 0 7494 6610 7 Paperback January 2013

Order online at **www.koganpage.com**

Find out more; visit **www.koganpage.com** and
sign up for offers and regular e-newsletters.

Also available from **Kogan Page**

ISBN: 978 0 7494 6590 2 Paperback September 2012

Order online at **www.koganpage.com**

Find out more; visit **www.koganpage.com** and
sign up for offers and regular e-newsletters.

Also available from **Kogan Page**

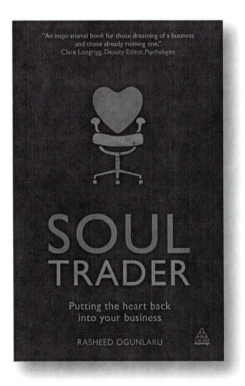

ISBN: 978 0 7494 6637 4 Paperback October 2012

Order online at **www.koganpage.com**

Find out more; visit **www.koganpage.com** and
sign up for offers and regular e-newsletters.

CPSIA information can be obtained at www.ICGtesting.com
Printed in the USA
BVOW03s2303060814

362003BV00003B/15/P

9 780749 468910